Disce Latinum

BOOK II

R. O. MARSH.

GW00455075

PUBLISHED BY MARIA PRICE
39 Kennedy Road, Shrewsbury, Shropshire

ISBN 978 0 952 186 182

PREFACE

Book II continues the story of Lucius Iulius Rufus, his wife Aemilia, his eldest son Marcus, aged twenty, and the twins, Tullus and Iulia, aged seven. The year is 82 A.D., later 83 and 84.

The following grammar is not introduced into English-Latin exercises:—Imperative, Ego, Tu, Hic, Ille, Is, Qui.

ACKNOWLEDGEMENTS

The Baths of Diocletian (page 17 & cover)   Alan Sorrell 'Imperial Rome'
(Lutterworth Press)
Roman Legion (page 84)   Peter Connolly 'Greece and Rome at War'
(Macdonald)
The other illustrations were drawn specially for this book.
Map of Britain (page 54)   Christopher Martin

Theatre	(page 4)	
Raeda	(page 76)	Angela Martin
Plaustrum	(page 76)	
Cisium	(page 77)	

Plan of Baths	(page 18)	
Roman Soldier	(page 25)	
Gladiators	(page 30)	
The Amphitheatre	(page 38)	Peter Lloyd
Plan of Camp	(page 62)	
Cohorts	(page 86)	

For background information I am indebted to all the usual sources. A list of recommended books can be found in the Teaching Notes.

1991 EDITION

As useful preparation for the new CE paper comprehension exercises have been included in chapters 13–23. This edition is still compatible with older editions.

1994 EDITION

In response to requests macrons have been added in the Latin—English vocabulary and in the boxed vocabularies; Latin sentences start with small letters; some other small changes have been made. In chapter 13 two pages have been added. All page numbers, chapter numbers and exercise numbers are the same and this edition is completely compatible with previous editions.

CONTENTS

CHAPTER 13

MYTHS AND LEGENDS

These are the stories of the gods and heroes of ancient Greece and Rome. There are other myths and legends from other parts of the world, for example the Norse stories of Woden and Thor and Beowulf.

They are called myths if they are about gods and they often try to explain things which seemed bewildering and frightening to simple people long ago. For example Jupiter's thunderbolts explain thunder and lightning, Proserpine's six months confinement in the Underworld explains winter.

If they are about heroes they are usually legends and they probably started as accounts of true adventures which were later altered and embroidered by story-tellers to make better stories.

Here is a list of the main gods and goddesses. Stories about them can be read in 'Men and Gods' by Rex Warner and in many other books.

GODS AND GODDESSES

Roman names	Greek names	Something about them
Saturnus (Saturn)	Kronos	Father of Jupiter, Crops.
Iuppiter (Jupiter)	Zeus	King of the Gods
Iuno (Juno)	Hera	Queen of the Gods
Neptunus (Neptune)	Poseidon	God of the Sea
Pluto, Dis	Pluto, Hades	King of the Underworld
Mars	Ares	War
Apollo	Apollo	Sun, Music, Prophecy
Diana	Artemis	Moon, Hunting, Animals
Venus	Aphrodite	Love, Beauty
Minerva	Athene	Wisdom, Arts and Crafts, War
Ceres	Demeter	Crops
Mercurius (Mercury)	Hermes	Messenger, Conductor of Souls
Cupido (Cupid)	Eros	Love
Vulcanus (Vulcan)	Hephaistos	Fire, Blacksmiths
Bacchus	Bacchus	Wine, Drama
Vesta	Hestia	Goddess of the Hearth
Pan, Faunus	Pan	Shepherds, Countryside
Iris	Iris	Messenger, Rainbow
Ianus (Janus)	—	Beginnings, Doorways

PERFECTS FORMED FROM IRREGULAR PRINCIPAL PARTS

Steti, feci, vidi, cepi and posui occur on the next page. If you have not yet learnt the principal parts, look in the vocabulary. If you can't find steti, look at all words starting st- and you will find sto. Similarly with the others.

THE STORY OF ARACHNE

Lydia is now part of western Turkey; it was then a separate kingdom.
Minerva was the goddess of arts and crafts.

erat olim puella Graeca, nomine Arachne, quae in Lydia habitabat.
haec puella telam cotidie texebat et picturas pulchras faciebat. amici
puellam saepe laudabant. 'quam pulchras picturas!' inquiunt. 'Minerva
ipsa non tam bene texit.'

    'ita vero,' inquit Arachne. 'Minerva ipsa non tam bene texit.'   5

    dum Arachne laborat, subito vetula domum intravit. picturam
intente inspexit. 'salve, Arachne,' inquit. 'quam pulchras picturas facis!
quam bene texis!'

    'ita vero,' respondit puella superba. 'nemo melius texit.'

    'nonne dea Minerva melius texit?' rogavit vetula.   10

    'minime,' clamavit Arachne. 'si Minerva melius texit, cur non ad
terram descendit et artem suam demonstrat? cur certamen vitat?'

Guess or look up:—picturas, intente, inspexit, descendit, artem.
quae = who, which. tela = web, cloth, loom. texo, texere, texui (3) = I weave.
ipsa = herself. tam = so. bene = well. vetula = old woman. superbus = proud.
nemo = nobody. melius = better. dea = goddess. certamen (N) = contest.

THE STORY OF ARACHNE (continued)

'Minerva certamen non vitat,' clamavit dea irata. non iam vetula ante
puellam stetit sed Minerva ipsa. 'para alteram telam et incipiemus.'

    diu dea et puella mortalis laboraverunt. Minerva texuit omnia bona
quae immortales fecerunt. Arachne tamen texuit omnia stulta et
ridicula quae immortales fecerunt. ubi hoc vidit, dea irata telam 5
laceravit et puellam radio suo iterum iterumque percussit. Arachne,
iam territa, funem cepit et circum collum suum posuit.

    'poenam morte non vitabis,' clamavit Minerva. 'pendebis sed vives et
semper texes.' statim puellam aqua magica sparsit et in araneam vertit.

Guess or look up:—mortalis, immortales, ridicula, laceravit, magica,
aranea.

alter = another	*poena = punishment*
incipio (3½) = I begin	*mors (mortis, F) = death*
omnia = all things	*pendeo (2) = I hang*
radius = shuttle	*vivo (3) = I live*
percutio, percutere, percussi = I	*spargo, spargere, sparsi = I sprinkle*
strike	*verto, vertere, verti = I turn*
funis (funis, M) = rope	
collum = neck	

THE ROMAN THEATRE

In early days theatres in Rome were temporary wooden stages with temporary wooden seats. The first permanent theatre was built on the Campus Martius in 55 B.C. Roman theatres were modelled on Greek theatres but with two differences. They were not built against the side of a hill usually and the semicircular area in front of the stage, called the ORCHESTRA, was not for the chorus to dance in but contained the best seats, reserved for senators. Behind and around rose the CAVEA, the main body of seats. The first fourteen rows were reserved for knights; for the other seats it was first come first served.

High up on each side, where the boxes are in a modern theatre, was a TRIBUNAL (literally = platform). On the one side it was reserved for priestesses; on the other for the man putting on the play and his assistants. Facing the audience was the SCAENA, the stage and its backcloth, though it was not a cloth but a permanent stone structure of two or three storeys with three doorways through it. Very often the stage represented a street scene and the doorways were the doors of three houses.

There were other big differences between Roman and modern theatres. Plays were acted in the daytime. The theatre was open to the sky, though awnings were sometimes erected. Plays were not put on every day but at festivals when shops were closed and business ceased. Admission was free. The curtain fell, rather than rose, to reveal the stage. The actors wore masks.

Roman theatres were large, holding up to 40,000 spectators. The masks helped the audience to recognize what characters the actors represented. They also had different clothes for different characters and different wigs—white for old men, black for young men, red for slaves.

As the performance lasted several hours, the audience brought food and drink with them and cushions for the hard stone seats. Attendants sprinkled perfumed water to make the theatre cooler and pleasanter.

Roman audiences liked comedies, especially those of Plautus and Terence. There were also mimes and pantomimes. Mimes were short sketches of daily life with much singing and dancing. In pantomimes one actor mimed the actions of an ancient myth while singers sang the story.

The Roman audience was a lively one: they frequently shouted and hissed. When several plays were competing for a prize, paid gangs of supporters clapped or hissed as directed, adding to the noise.

13 A.   **MOSTELLARIA**

Today Lucius has taken his wife to the theatre where there is a performance of 'Mostellaria' ('The Haunted House') by the old playwright, Plautus, who lived about 200 B.C.

The scene is a street in Athens. We join the play in Act II. Theopropides has been abroad on business for three years. Meanwhile his son Philolaches spends his time in the family house drinking and feasting with his friend Callidamates and his own slave Tranio. There is also with him Philematium, a pretty slave-girl whom he has fallen in love with and bought and set free.

Their pleasures are interrupted by the unexpected return of the father. Tranio has just seen him down at the harbour while buying provisions. Their first impulse is to leave the house but Callidamates is helplessly drunk and cannot move. Tranio suggests that they stay where they are, absolutely silent. He will shut up the house, lock it from the outside and when the father arrives, tell him that it has been shut up for a year because it is haunted.

[Enter Theopropides. Tranio is watching]

THEO quam laetus domum meam video! quam laetus familiam
      meam videbo! filius me non exspectat. quam laetus me
      videbit!

TRAN quam laetus te videbit!
[aside]

THEO quid est hoc? quis ianuam clausit? pulsabo.   5
      heus! numquis ianuam aperiet?
                     [Tranio shows himself]

TRAN quis prope domum nostram venit?

THEO ecce! hic est servus meus, Tranio.

TRAN o Theopropides, o domine, salve! valesne?

THEO valeo. sed vos? insanine estis? cur in via habitatis? cur   10
      domum clausistis? cur nemo ianuam aperit? cur nemo
      respondet? diu pulsavi.

TRAN tetigistine?

THEO tetigi et pulsavi.

TRAN eheu!   15

THEO quid est?

TRAN fecisti malum.

THEO quid?

TRAN fuge! discede ab ianua! fuge ad me! tetigistine ianuam?

THEO quomodo pulsavi si non tetigi?   20

TRAN necavisti—

THEO necavi?

TRAN totam familiam tuam.

THEO quomodo? cur? quid mihi subito dicis?

TRAN abhinc unum annum domo discessimus. ex eo tempore nemo 25
      domum intravit.

THEO cur? dic mihi!

TRAN circumspecta! numquis nos audit?

THEO nemo.

TRAN circumspecta iterum!   30

THEO nemo est, dico. narra mihi totam rem!

TRAN capitale scelus hic factum est.

THEO quid dicis?

TRAN hospes hospitem necavit.

THEO necavit?   35

TRAN pecuniamque hospitis cepit corpusque hic defodit.

THEO quomodo de hoc audivisti?

pulso = I knock	*eo = that*
heus = Hey	*tempus (temporis) = time*
numquis = Won't anyone	*numquis = is anyone*
valeo = I am well	*rem = thing*
nemo = no one	*scelus = crime*
malus = bad	*factum est = has been committed*
quomodo = how	*hospes (hospitis) = host, guest*
dico = I say, tell	*defodio = I bury*
abhinc = ago	

TRAN	mortuus ad filium tuum in somnis venit.
	(The door rattles)
THEO	st! st!
TRAN	quid est?
THEO	ianua concrepuit.
TRAN	mortuusne ianuam movit?
THEO	timeo. timeo. mortuus venit.

                             (Tapping noise)

TRAN   stulti! fabulam meam conturbabunt.
(to himself)

           (Theopropides approaches the door)
       discede ab ianua! fuge! fuge!
          (Theopropides starts to flee but stops)

THEO	quo fugiam? cur tu non fugis?
TRAN	non timeo.

           (Whisper from inside: 'heus! heus!')

(to himself)
       o stulti! quid faciet dominus meus, ubi fabulam falsam
         invenerit? timeo.
          (Whisper from inside: 'heus! Tranio!')

(in whisper to voice inside)
       non me vocabis, si sapis.
(loudly to door)
       innocens sum. innocens sum. non ego ianuam pulsavi.

THEO	cui hoc dicis?
TRAN	mortuus clamavit quod tu ianuam pulsavisti. sed cur non
	fugis?

       (Louder, impatient rattle. Theopropides starts to flee)

TRAN	fuge! fuge! tege caput! voca deos!
THEO	Hercules, te voco. *(exit)*
TRAN	o Hercules, ego quoque te voco. quid faciet dominus meus si
	verum invenerit?

                   (exit other side)

mortuus = the dead man	*cui = to whom*
in somnis = in a dream	*tego = I cover*
concrepo = I rattle	*caput = head*
conturbo = I spoil	*deus = god*
quo = where (to)	*verum = the truth*
sapio = I am wise	

For the moment the situation is saved but in the next scene, while Tranio and Theopropides are talking, a money-lender interrupts them looking for Philolaches who owes him interest on the money he borrowed to buy the slave-girl. When the father asks Tranio why his son borrowed money, the slave pretends it was to buy another house. Then, of course, the father wants to look round the house and Tranio has to pile deception on deception.

Eventually Theopropides finds out everything and Tranio runs to an altar for refuge. Finally Callidamates, who is now sober, persuades the father to pardon both his son and his slave.

VOCABULARY 13

lēo (leōnis, M)	= lion	deus	= god
dux (ducis, C)	= leader	malus	= bad
vōx (vōcis, F)	= voice	maneō (2)	= I remain
soror (sorōris, F)	= sister	dīcō (3)	= I say, tell
princeps (principis, C)	= chief	tegō (3)	= I cover
māter (mātris, F)	= mother	relinquō (3)	= I leave
frāter (frātris, M)	= brother	nēmō	= no one
tempus (temporis, N)	= time	quō?	= where to?
caput (capitis, N)	= head	quōmodo?	= how?
flūmen (flūminis, N)	= river	ibi	= there

Exercise 13 X Questions about 13 B, lines 12–20.

1. What does Lamachus suggest in line 12? (2)
2. What did his men then do (lines 13–14)? (3)
3. What did Lamachus say after they'd left the city (15–16)? (3)
4. What did he request in lines 16–17? (1)
5. What was his men's reaction (18)? What did Lamachus then do? (3)
6. What did his men do with the body (lines 19–20)? (3)

GOLDEN STORIES

The Latin for a play is 'fabula', the same word as for a story. There were in those days, and still are in some parts of the world, professional storytellers who attracted crowds in public places and for a small charge told stories. 'Assem para et accipe auream fabulam' (Produce a coin and receive a golden story). Many of these stories are recounted by Lucius Apuleius in his book 'The Golden Ass'. The most famous is the story of Cupid and Psyche. Here is a much shorter one about Lamachus and his band robbing a house in the Greek city of Thebes.

13 B   THE STORY OF LAMACHUS

ubi ad urbem Thebas venimus, statim de fortunis mercatorum quaerebamus. mox de sene, nomine Chrysero, audivimus qui multam pecuniam habebat sed, quod erat avarus, domum parvam solus habitabat. itaque, ubi nox venit, ad ianuam senis festinavimus.

erat in ianua foramen magnum, clavi factum. in hoc foramen dux   5
noster Lamachus manum suam inmisit et claustrum movebat. Chryserus tamen nos audivit et ad ianuam magno silentio appropinquavit. subito clavo magno manum ducis nostri ad postem ianuae fixit. inde ad fenestram cucurrit et magna voce clamavit: 'subvenite! subvenite! domus mea ardet. mox tuae quoque ardebunt.'   10
quid faciemus? ducemne nostrum relinquemus an contra multos et iratos Thebanos pugnabimus? statim dux noster 'abscide,' inquit 'manum meam.' manum igitur gladiis abscidimus ibique in ianua reliquimus, ceterum Lamachum celeriter removimus.

postquam ex urbe fugimus, clamavit: 'si procedam, vos retardabo; si   15
hic manebo, Thebani me capient. necate me, si me amatis. liberate me

qui = who	claustrum = bolt
avarus = miser	clavus = nail
solus = alone	vox (vocis, F) = voice
foramen = hole	ardeo = I am on fire
clavis = key (many keys in those	relinquo (relinquere, reliqui) = I
days were big, clumsy	leave
things)	an = or
factum = made	abscido = I cut off
manus (F) = hand	maneo = I remain

9

dolore et captivitate. laetus ero si gladius amici me necabit.' ubi nos
haesitantes vidit, gladio suo pectus subito transfixit. corpus ducis nostri
veste nova diligenter teximus et in flumen coniecimus. requiescat in
pace.   20

- *dolor = pain*
- *haesitantes = hesitating*
- *pectus (pectoris, N) = chest*

flumen (fluminis, N) = river
requiescat = may he rest
pax (pacis, F) = peace

FABLES

Another type of story is the fable, and the word 'fable' comes from the
Latin 'fabula'. The most famous collection of fables is Aesop's. He was
born in Phrygia in about 570 BC. At first he was a slave but later worked
for Croesus, king of Lydia. How many fables he collected and how many
he wrote himself is uncertain. Many of Aesop's Fables were retold in
Latin in verse by Phaedrus, a slave from Thrace who was set free by the
Emperor Augustus. The fable below is a simplified version.

13 C.   THE WOLF AND THE LAMB

olim agnus, qui aquam quaerebat, ad flumen parvum venit. in ripa
fluminis stabat superior lupus. statim lupus, qui iurgium cupiebat, haec
verba dixit:
   'bibo. cur aquam turbulentam mihi fecisti?'
   agnus timidus 'quomodo,' inquit 'hoc potest, domine? nam aqua a te   5
ad me currit.'
   repulsus his verbis veris lupus primo tacuit. inde:
   'anno proximo mihi male dixisti.'
   respondit agnus 'natus non eram.'
   'si non tu, certe frater tuus mihi male dixit.'   10
   'fratres non habeo, domine.'
   'tace!' clamavit lupus. 'pater tuus mihi male dixit.'
   itaque agnum statim necavit et devoravit.
Aesopus hanc fabulam hominibus malis scripsit qui homines
innocentes causis falsis opprimunt.   15

agnus = lamb
ripa = bank
superior = upstream
lupus = wolf
iurgium = quarrel
turbulentus = muddy

potest = is possible
repulsus = repulsed
proximus = last
male = rude things
certe = certainly
opprimo = I oppress

PERFECTS FORMED FROM IRREGULAR PRINCIPAL PARTS

Where a verb has irregular principal parts these are given in the vocabulary.

The third principal part is the 1st. person singular of the perfect. For example from DO it is DEDI (=I have given) and the tense goes:—
DEDI, DEDISTI, DEDIT, DEDIMUS, DEDISTIS, DEDERUNT.

Exercise 13 D

What is the Latin for:— I have moved, I have wept, I have opened, I have made, I have fallen?

Now write out the whole tense of any two of these.

Exercise 13 E

1. vidimus.
2. risit.
3. dedisti.
4. cepimus.
5. rexit.
6. clausistis.
7. cucurrerunt.
8. stetit.
9. veni.
10. tetigisti.
11. They laughed.
12. He has run.
13. She sat.
14. He has seen.
15. He has departed.
16. They did not come.
17. I led.
18. We haven't played.
19. He threw a spear.
20. You have not worked.

Exercise 13 F *(A mixture of tenses. The Present, Future and Imperfect are formed from the first Principal Part; the Perfect from the third.)*

1. pecuniam dabant.
2. reget.
3. cur risisti?
4. currebant.
5. pueri sedent.
6. librum scripsit.
7. pecuniam mittam.
8. quid cupiebat?
9. cur timetis?
10. quid dedisti?
11. He will lead.
12. I did not swim.
13. She was listening.
14. They have seen.
15. You have not written.
16. I shall fortify the town.
17. We shall give a gift.
18. You used to laugh.
19. He sent his son.
20. Have you touched the food?

ADJECTIVES AND THIRD DECLENSION NOUNS

It is more difficult to make adjectives (like Bonus, Niger, Tener) agree with Third Declension nouns, since they do not rhyme.
Until you can do it easily, you must go through a careful process.
Example: 'We have a good king.'
Always translate the noun first: 'Regem'.
Now to make bonus agree, write on a piece of rough paper: regem—acc., sing., masc.
Now find that part of bonus—bonum.

Example: 'of our king'
   regis—gen., sing., masc.—nostri.

Example: 'in our cities'
   in urbibus—abl., plur., fem—nostris.

Exercise 13 G

(a) Make bonus agree with:—
    matris, rege, ducum, iuveni, vocem, nomen, nomina, soror, militibus, principes.

(b) Translate these phrases in the case indicated. Do the noun first and then the adjective.
 1. long night (acc.)
 2. angry lions (gen.)
 3. new songs (nom.)
 4. big city (abl.)
 5. many leaders (nom.)
 6. great king (voc.)
 7. your head (acc.)
 8. great fear (abl.)
 9. long names (acc.)
 10. happy mothers (dat.)

(c) In what case is each phrase? If it can be more than one case, name all:—
 1. vocem tuam.
 2. flumina magna.
 3. hoc tempore.
 4. pedibus nigris.
 5. senex stultus.
 6. milites fessi.
 7. magnum opus.
 8. regum nostrorum.
 9. hominis stulti.
 10. patri meo.

THE IMPERATIVE

The Imperative is the part of the verb used for giving orders:
audi, puer   = Listen, boy.
audite, pueri   = Listen, boys.
Imperatives have come occasionally throughout the book but there are far more in 'Mostellaria'. They can be recognized because they normally end in vowels. In this book there are often exclamation marks to help you.

Singular: AMA	MONE	REGE	CAPE	AUDI
Plural: AMATE	MONETE	REGITE	CAPITE	AUDITE

Exercise 13 H

1. sedete, pueri! tacete, pueri!
2. festina in cubiculum tuum, Marce!
3. subveni! subveni! caupo me necabit.
4. fugite, mei amici! Galli urbem ceperunt.
5. da mihi cibum! da mihi vinum!

Exercise 13 I

1. The old-man fears the long nights.
2. He has given water to the tired soldiers.
3. The slaves have done many tasks.
4. I have heard the voice of my father.
5. The chiefs of the Gauls have fled.
6. The chief's son has given the signal.
7. They have captured our leader.
8. The stupid merchants have not sent the money.
9. They have covered the body of the dead chief.
10. She loves her brother; he loves his sister.

Exercise 13 J

1. tace, Tite! quam stultus es!
2. duos oculos nigros mox habebis.
3. principes Gallorum milites ibi celaverunt.
4. postquam haec verba dixit, discessit.
5. gladium telumque filio meo dedi.
6. periculum vidit auxiliumque misit.

OTHER EXERCISES

Exercise 13 K   Questions about 13 A.

1. In what case is:— familiam (line 1), me (2), domum (7), domine (9), via (10)?
2. In what tense is:— videbo (2), exspectat (2), clausit (5), aperiet (6), pulsavi (12)?
3. What part of speech is:—ianuam (5), prope (7), est (8), meus (8), vos (10)?

Exercise 13 L   Translate into Latin:—

Once I used to live in the city. My master's house was big but evil. When night came, I never used to sleep. I used to hear noises. The other slaves also heard noises. We used to hear chains. The chains approached slowly. Then an old-man entered the hall. Once I saw the old man from my bedroom. He had long hair and a long beard. The ghost frightened my master very-much. Eventually he killed my master. Then I and the other slaves fled from the city.

Exercise 13 M More Practice at Perfects.

1. discesserunt.
2. stetimus.
3. non lusit.
4. silvam reliquimus.
5. Marcum misi.
6. cur non scripsisti?
7. saxa coniecerunt.
8. librum aperuit.
9. pecuniam tetigisti.
10. cibum ibi posui.
11. He did not write.
12. We placed the table.
13. They have sent a slave.
14. He has opened the gate.
15. You left your friends.
16. She has seen the garden.
17. I have slept.
18. We have moved the books.
19. What have you done?
20. Why have you come?

Exercise 13 N

1. What are the six cases? Spell them correctly.
2. Which case means TO?
3. Which case means OF?
4. Which case means BY?
5. Which examples in the Grammar do these nouns decline like:—donum, oculus, lux, porta, corpus?
6. In which cases are these words:—muros, locus, lucem, mercatoris, librum, sagittarum, amice, periculi, portam, nomine?
7. What TWO cases can cibo be? And mensis? And miles?
8. What THREE cases can each of these be:—filia, domini, corpora?
9. Which ending of Mensa can be FOUR different cases?

Exercise 13 O Practice at the Genitive.

Reword the phrases in English, then translate them into Latin, as shown in the example.

Example: Marcus' father = the father of Marcus = pater Marci OR Marci pater.

1. The boy's book.
2. The girl's eyes.
3. The soldiers' stories.
4. The soldier's stories.
5. The friend's gifts.
6. The friends' gifts.
7. The chief's son.
8. The horses' food.

Exercise 13 P Jumbled Words.

1. ALLEC—spiders in store here.
2. ONE PATCH—empty tomb.
3. LICET—found in both triclinium and cubiculum.
4. SEA CAN—where actors strut.
5. LIP COAT—twin peak with the Arx.
6. LASER—they have their shrine in the atrium.
7. SIR LEG—small and furry and eaten by Romans.
8. CHEST ROAR—no music here, but the best seats.

CHAPTER 14

A SENATORIAL CAREER

During the Empire the citizens still voted for the magistrates but the surest way of being elected was to be recommended by the Emperor (IMPERATOR). Only the sons of senators could hope to become senators themselves except for a few chosen by the Emperor.

The first step in a senatorial career was to serve for one or two years as a tribune (TRIBUNUS) with a legion. Returning to Rome you then became a VIGINTIVIR, one of twenty minor magistrates. You then stood for the quaestorship and became a senator. At regular intervals after this you could hold the other magistracies mentioned in Chapter 6 (aedile, praetor, consul). With the Emperor's favour your promotion could be accelerated.

When he joined his legion, the senator's son was a Tribunus Laticlavius and senior to the other five tribunes who were from Equestrian families (Knights) and served for ten years.

14 A	A POST IN BRITAIN	
TUL	ducesne me ad amphitheatrum, Marce? mox erit spectaculum.	
MARC	eheu! ante spectaculum gladiatorium ego ad Britanniam discessero.	
TUL	quot annos in Britannia manebis?	
MARC	duos annos manebo. ubi revenero, vigintivir ero, inde quaestor.	5
MAT	si populus Romanus te quaestorem creaverit.	
PAT	si Imperator te commendaverit.	
TUL	ego te non commendabo. crudelissimus es.	
MARC	(ridet) quod araneas neco?	10
TUL	quod multa animalia necas. eum canem sagittis necavisti.	
PAT	is canis erat rabidus, Tulle.	
MARC	in Britannia multos Britannos necabo. nonne id erit crudelissimum?	
TUL	minime. Britanni scuta et gladios habent. se defendent. fortasse Britanni te necabunt.	15

spectaculum = a show
creo = I elect
populus = people
crudelissimus = very cruel

canis, scutum, defendo, vinco,
  occido—see Boxed Vocab
rabidus = mad
se = themselves

MAT	eheu! quid dixisti, Tulle? nemo Marcum necabit. fortasse
	Agricola bellum iam confecit.
MARC	Agricola Ordovices vicit; Druidas, qui in insulam Monam
	fugerunt, occidit; iam bellum contra Caledonios parat.
MAT	fortasse Caledonios vicerit, antequam venies.
MARC	o mater, miles iam sum. milites bella non timent. si
	Agricola bellum confecerit, quomodo gloriam capiam?

20

Agricola—governor of Britain
Ordovices = the Ordovices, (a tribe
in North Wales)

qui = who
Mona = Anglesey
antequam = before

VOCABULARY 14

populus	= people	is	= that, he
scūtum	= shield	nāvigō (1)	= I sail
pēs (pedis, M)	= foot	creō (1)	= I elect
homō (hominis, C)	= man	vincō (3)	= I conquer
pater (patris, M)	= father	occīdō (3)	= I kill
opus (operis, N)	= work	dēfendō (3)	= I defend
carmen (carminis, N)	= song	accipiō (3½)	= I receive
canis (canis, M)	= dog	tam	= so

Exercise 14 X Questions about 14 A, lines 13–23.

1. Why does Tullus not think that killing Britons is cruel (lines 15–16). Answer fully. (3)
2. Why is Aemilia, Marcus' mother, upset (line 17)? (3)
3. Who defeated the Ordovices? (1)
4. Where did the Druids take refuge? Were they safe there? (2)
5. What does Aemilia hope will happen before her son reaches Scotland (21)? (2)
6. What is Marcus' reaction to his mother's hopes and fears (22–23)? Answer fully. (4)

ROMAN BATHS

Almost all towns had Baths (Thermae); in Rome itself there were more than eight hundred eventually. These were not swimming baths nor ordinary washing baths but large buildings where you could not only wash and bathe but also sunbathe, exercise, sweat, be massaged and above all meet your friends and chat.

In the country those who could afford them had their own suite of baths at home, but in the town they liked to join their friends. Baths were usually open from noon to sunset but most people had lunch at noon, then took a siesta, then went to the Baths at 2.0 p.m. or after. The entrance fee was small and children were admitted free. There were separate baths for men and women.

The main rooms at the Baths were:—

(1) APODYTERIUM (changing room), in which there were stone benches and in the wall niches where you left your clothes. One of your slaves guarded them or you tipped a bathhouse slave to look after them.

(2) TEPIDARIUM (warm room).

17

(3) CALDARIUM (hot room) with a hot bath at one end and a basin of cool water at the other.

(4) FRIGIDARIUM (cold room) with a cold plunge bath.

There were also usually:—

(5) PALAESTRA (exercise ground), a sandy, out of doors area, surrounded by colonnades, where you could play catch, wrestle, fence or sunbathe.

(6) PISCINA (swimming pool).

Both the water and the rooms were heated by a furnace burning charcoal. Hot air circulated under the floors and between the walls, providing an even heat. This heating system was called a HYPOCAUST.

Soap had not been invented and although soda took its place for some things, olive oil was favoured by bathers. To remove oil and the dirt you scraped yourself (or had your slave scrape you) with a STRIGIL (metal scraper).

All this was done at a leisurely pace while chatting to your friends. Pedlars walked round selling snacks.

The picture on page 17 is of the great hall at the Baths of Diocletian. These vast baths covered 27 acres and were the most splendid in the world. Spread among the various rooms three thousand people could use them at the same time. They were not typical but a provincial coming to Rome and using them would recognize the lay-out of the rooms.

Below is a plan of a smaller, more normal baths.

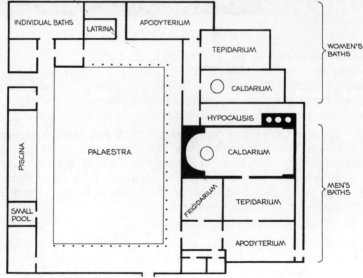

PLAN OF A TYPICAL SMALL TOWN BATHS
BASED ON THE STABIAN BATHS IN POMPEII

NOTICE THAT THE HYPOCAUSIS (COMMONLY CALLED 'HYPOCAUST') IS PLACED BETWEEN THE TWO HOT ROOMS TO MINIMIZE THE DISSIPATION OF HEAT.

AT THE BATHS

Marcus ad Thermas Agrippae cotidie veniebat. nam amici quoque eius ad eas thermas veniebant.

primum apodyterium intravit et vestes cum servo reliquit. inde corpus suum oleo unxit et in palaestram festinavit. multos amicos ibi invenit.   5

MARC   salve, Aule. salve, Alexander.
AUL   salve, Marce. cur tam laetus es hodie?
ALEX   fortasse amicus noster cum Flavia iterum ambulavit.
MARC   laetus sum quod mox ero miles. mox ero tribunus sub
          Agricola. pater meus epistolam ab eo hodie accepit. mox   10
          igitur in Britanniam iter faciam.
AUL   in Britanniam! quam longum iter!
ALEX   o miserum Marcum! Britanni sunt barbari! corpora sua vitro
          inficiunt. caeruleus revenies!
AUL   Venetus reveniet! Marcus qui Albatos semper amavit!   15
MARC   sed multas terras et multos homines videbo.
AUL   et multas puellas. scribe ad me de puellis.
ALEX   fortasse captivas e Britannia reduces. fortasse ancillas nobis
          capies.
MARC   fortasse. primum tamen nos exercere necesse est.   20
AUL   ita vero. tempus est corpora exercere.

cotidie iuvenes, postquam se exercuerunt, in tepidarium procedebant, inde in caldarium. ibi sedebant et diu sudabant. postquam satis sudaverunt, in tepidarium reveniebant, ubi servi oleum et strigiles parabant. servi corpora iuvenum oleo unguebant et 25 strigilibus radebant. Inde Marcus et amici in frigidarium procedebant et in aquam frigidam descendebant. quam delectabat eos!

tam = so	*caeruleus = blue*
accipio = I receive	*reduco = I bring back*
oleum = oil	*exercere = to exercise*
ungueo = I smear	*se = themselves*
vitrum = woad	*sudo = I sweat*
inficio = I dye	*rado = I scrape*

THE FUTURE PERFECT (Grammar page 19)

This is formed from the Third Principal Part. For example: AUDIVI gives AUDIVERO (the -i being dropped and the -ero added.)
DEDI gives DEDERO (DEDERIS, DEDERIT, DEDERIMUS, DEDERITIS, DEDERINT).
Note: the endings are the same for all conjugations.

Exercise 14 C

1. ambulaverit.
2. vicero.
3. moverint.
4. discesseritis.
5. pugnaverint.
6. portam clausero.
7. urbem reliquerint.
8. manserit.
9. revenerimus.
10. audiveritis.

Exercise 14 D

1. I shall have moved.
2. I shall have slept.
3. I shall have sailed.
4. I shall have seen.
5. I shall have left.
6. I shall have stood.
7. I shall have fled.
8. I shall have sent.
9. I shall have written.
10. I shall have walked.
11. We shall have prepared.
12. They will have remained.
13. He will have written.
14. We shall have departed.
15. He will have fled.
16. They will have run.
17. He will have sailed.
18. You will have seen.
19. He will have laughed.
20. They will have come.

IS (= THAT, HE, SHE, IT) (Grammar page 12)

(1) Is = That, E.g. eam puellam amo.
   Marcus est filius eius senatoris.
(2) Is also means He (that man), She (that woman),
   It (that thing). E.g. eam amo = I love her.
   id dabo = I shall give it. eum timeo = I fear him.
(3) The genitive Eius = His (of him) and the genitive plural Eorum
   (or Earum) = Their (of them).
   E.g. eius filius = the son of him = his son.
   eorum urbs = the city of them = their city.

Exercise 14 E

1. in ea urbe habito.
2. rex eos laudavit.
3. eum miserunt.
4. eius canis est mortuus.
5. vinum ei non dabo.
6. id carmen me delectat.
7. eius caput est magnum.
8. cum ea semper ambulat.
9. id ad te mittam.
10. eorum soror est Iulia.

Exercise 14 F

1. nonne ea carmina regem delectaverint?
2. multos homines in urbe vidi.
3. id opus ante noctem confecero.
4. si cupis, te ad theatrum ducam.
5. eius frater id carmen non amat.
6. inter flumen et oppidum erat parva silva.
7. vocem tuam non audiverint.
8. cur non festinas, Aule? tempus fugit.

Exercise 14 G (If 'have' = 'possess', use 'habeo').

1. Julia has called our father.
2. My brothers have big feet.
3. Our sister has a big head.
4. The boys have left clothes on the field.
5. He will not have received the letter, Marcus.
6. The girls will have sung many songs.
7. Melissa sings with a beautiful voice.
8. The Roman people will conquer the Gauls.

OTHER EXERCISES

Exercise 14 H   Questions about 14 A.

1. What part of speech is:— me (1), ad (1), eheu (2), annos (4), manebis (4)?
2. In what case is:— canem (11), sagittis (11), Tulle (17), bellum (18), miles (22)?
3. In what tense is:— duces (1), discessero (3), es (9), neco (10), necavisti (11)?
4. Give an English word derived from:— annos (4), duos (5), populus (7), creaverit (7), multa (11).
5. What do you know about the Druids?
6. How far do you agree with Tullus' views on killing?

Exercise 14 I

1. I shall remain and defend the king.
2. I have received a letter from your father.
3. Melissa delights men with songs and stories.
4. Have you finished the jobs, Tullus?
5. He will have hidden the body.
6. Why have you covered your heads? (*tuus or vester?*)

Exercise 14 J   Vocabulary Revision.

1. itaque discessit.
2. postea revenit.
3. quid dixit?
4. quo fugit?
5. celeriter cucurri.
6. procul ab eo steti.
7. postridie scripsi.
8. lente ambulavisti.
9. satis dixisti.
10. me paene occidisti.

Exercise 14 K

After about ten minutes of revision divide into pairs and ask each other questions about:—
Life after Death, Slaves and Freedmen, Baths, Theatres.

CHAPTER 15

AFTER THE BATHS

Marcus et Aulus, postquam e thermis discesserunt, per ripam Tiberis
ambulabant.

'quam calidum est!' inquit Aulus. 'nonne flumen nos vocat? aqua nos
refrigerabit.'

'ego in flumine non natabo,' respondit Marcus. 'aqua est sordida. e 5
thermis modo venimus.'

subito voces audiverunt. tres nautae e taberna veniebant et carmen
novum cantabant.

'ecce taberna!' clamavit Marcus. 'nonne taberna nos vocat?'

'verum dicis. taberna nos vocat. vinum nos refrigerabit.'   10

tabernam igitur intraverunt vinumque mox bibebant. subito miles
ebrius intravit et cauponi 'da mihi vinum!' clamavit. 'calidus sum.'

'ubi est pecunia?' rogavit caupo.

'hodie pecuniam non habeo,' respondit miles. 'cras eam tibi dabo.'

'nulla pecunia, nullum vinum.'   15

miles ad Marcum se vertit. 'quis es?' inquit. 'quid est nomen tuum?'

'sum Marcus Iulius Rufus.'

'nonne tu pecuniam mihi dabis? tu senatoris filius es. itaque multam
pecuniam habes.'

Marcus 'iuvenes,' respondit 'multam pecuniam numquam habent. 20
unum tamen vini poculum tibi emam.'

miles, postquam vinum bibit, ad Aulum se vertit et 'nonne tu,' inquit
'poculum vini mihi emes? calidus sum. vinum me refrigerabit.'

'satis bibisti,' inquit Marcus.

'nimis bibisti,' inquit caupo.   25

'ebrius es,' inquit Aulus.

'ebrius? id non verum est. cur me insultas?'

miles ad Aulum ruit sed ebrius ad pedes eius cecidit. Aulus risit et
vinum suum in caput militis infudit. 'ecce vinum!' inquit. 'vinum te
refrigerabit.'   30

miles iratus stetit iterumque ad Aulum ruit. inde Marcus et Aulus
militem ceperunt et e taberna portaverunt.

ripa = bank	*se vertit = turned*
calidus = hot	*poculum = cup*
modo = just	*emo = I buy*
ebrius = drunk	*nimis = too much*
caupo = innkeeper	*infudit = poured*
nullus = no	

'ad flumen!' clamavit Marcus.

hominem ad Tiberim portaverunt et in aquam coniecerunt.

'iam satis bibes!' clamavit Aulus.

'aqua te refrigerabit!' clamavit Marcus.

35

VOCABULARY 15

galea	= helmet	quī	= who / which
rīpa	= bank		
avus	= grandfather	sōlus	= only / alone
arma (2,N,plural)	= arms		
pāx (pācis, F)	= peace	nūllus	= no / none
cōnsul (cōnsulis, M)	= consul		
custōs (custōdis, M)	= guard	legō (3)	= I read / I choose
virtūs (virtūtis, F)	= courage		
onus (oneris, N)	= burden	emō (3)	= I buy
		trahō (3)	= I drag

---

15 B   THE DAY OF DEPARTURE

iam dies venerat. Marcus, qui iter longum numquam solus fecerat, erat laetus sed trepidus.

atrium erat plenum armorum quae pater ei comparaverat. erant duo pila, gladius, pugio. erat lorica quam Marci avus olim gesserat. erat galea nova quam amici Marco dederant. multae vestes in atrio erant 5 quas ancillae fecerant; multae quoque quas mater emerat. in cella erat magna copia cibi quem coquus paraverat.

iam servi onera in mulis ponebant. iam servus equum, quem pater Marco dederat, ad ianuam ducebat. iam tempus erat valedicere. tota familia erat in atrio. multae ancillae flebant. Marcus primum servis, 10 inde Tullo, postremo parentibus valedixit. Iulia, quae erat aegra, non erat in atrio. Marcus in eius cubiculum 'vale!' clamavit.

'vale!' respondit Iulia.

Marcus equum ascendit et per viam equitavit. servi mulos ducebant. semel se vertit et 'vale!' clamavit, inde per Portam Flaminiam discessit. 15 non flevit. miles erat.

dies	= day	avus	= grandfather
solus	= alone	galea	= helmet
trepidus	= anxious	copia	= quantity
arma	= arms	onus (oneris)	= burden
comparo	= I collect	valedicere	= to say goodbye
pilum	= spear	postremo	= lastly
pugio	= dagger	semel	= once
lorica	= breastplate	se vertit	= turned

GALEA = HELMET

LORICA = BREASTPLATE

GLADIUS = SWORD (a short, two-edged stabbing sword.)

PUGIO = DAGGER

SCUTUM = SHIELD (a rectangular shield, curved to fit the body. It was made of plywood covered with leather and had metal rims and boss.)

PILUM = SPEAR (The soldier had two of these. Each was seven feet long including an iron head of two feet. The point and the socket, where it joined the shaft, were hard, the other metal part soft. It bent when it struck an enemy shield.

CALIGAE = SANDALS

He wore a woollen tunic and a leather belt from which hung his dagger and an apron of metal discs on leather straps.

> # THE PLUPERFECT (Grammar page 19).
>
> This is formed from the Third Principal Part. For example: AUDIVI gives AUDIVERAM (the -i being dropped and -eram added). The endings are the same for all conjugations.

Exercise 15 C

1. laboraverant.
2. fugeras.
3. steteramus.
4. diu tacueram.
5. vicerant.
6. non reveneratis.

Exercise 15 D

1. I had swum.
2. I had slept.
3. I had seen.
4. I had stood.
5. I had run.
6. I had remained.
7. We had walked.
8. You had departed.
9. He had fled.
10. They had laughed.
11. We had conquered.
12. He had bought a dog.

Exercise 15 E PRACTICE AT ALL SIX TENSES

Remember which principal part is used.

REGO	REGERE	REXI	RECTUM

pres. fut. imperf.   perf. fut.perf. pluperf.

1. stant.
2. stabunt.
3. stabant.
4. steterant.
5. quid mones?
6. current.
7. quid misisti?
8. discesserint.
9. fugerunt.
10. cur rides?
11. They were calling.
12. You have come back.
13. We shall move.
14. You were listening.
15. I have won.
16. He used to work.
17. She will come.
18. I shall have remained.
19. He wants the money.
20. She had departed.

Exercise 15 F

1. puella, quae flebat, in flumen ceciderat.
2. montes, per quos iter facimus, sunt Alpes.
3. urbs quam videtis est Roma.
4. hi sunt pueri quorum vestes sunt sordidae.
5. hic est senator cuius filium servavisti.
6. quis tela cepit quae hic posui?
7. mercator cui pecuniam dedi fugit.
8. ubi sunt silvae in quibus ludebamus?

Exercise 15 G   (General Practice)

1. leo hominem miserum in silvam traxerat.
2. custodes qui regem defendunt sunt mortui.
3. nulli corporis custodes regem hodie comitant.
4. nonne opus fecisti? nox venit.
5. populus Romanus te consulem non creabit.
6. id est flumen in quo natamus.
7. Caledonios numquam vincetis.
8. nonne libros legisti quos tibi dedi?
9. quomodo haec onera portabunt?
10. milites vestros magnopere laudaverat.

Exercise 15 H

1. My sister will have read the letter <u>immediately.</u>
2. <u>How slowly</u> you walk! Mother is waiting.
3. I had <u>never</u> seen <u>so</u> small a dog.
4. <u>At-length</u> we came to a big river.
5. You will <u>not</u> have written the letters <u>in-vain.</u>
6. Your soldiers fought with great courage.

OTHER EXERCISES

Exercise 15 I Translate into Latin:—

When I heard about the ghost, I immediately rented the house. By night I sat alone in the study and wrote letters. Soon I heard a noise. The noise came into the hall, then into the study. When I looked-round, I saw the ghost. The ghost walked slowly through the study and proceeded into the courtyard. There it disappeared.

Exercise 15 J

1. The big dogs had dragged the man into the wood.
2. They had fortified the new city with a wall.
3. We shall defend our island. We shall soon win.
4. They killed the guards and captured the king.
5. He had not bought new arms for his son.
6. You read slowly but you write quickly.

Exercise 15 K ODD MAN OUT

Which word in each of the following eight groups of words is the Odd Man Out?

Example: spina, carceres, cenaculum, quadrigae. 'Cenaculum' is the odd one because it means 'a flat' while the others are all to do with the Circus.

Another example: amicus, onus, cibus, hortus. 'Onus' is the odd one because it is neuter and declines like 'Opus'.

1. triclinium, tablinum, piscina, culina, atrium.
2. apples, pineapples, pears, plums, cherries.
3. porta, bella, mensa, sagitta, puella.
4. Purpurei, Albati, Russati, Prasini, Veneti.
5. Hibernia, Graecia, Hispania, Britannia.
6. toga virilis, tunica laticlavia, stola.
7. apodyterium, tepidarium, frigidarium, lararium.
8. filia, silva, fossa, pecunia, nauta.

Exercise 15 L Questions about 15 B

1. Name seven different things (paragraph 2) which were prepared for Marcus to take with him? (7)
2. Where did the slaves put the baggage (line 8)? (1)
3. Where did Marcus say goodbye to people? Who was missing and why? (3)
4. Name four different people or groups to whom Marcus said goodbye? (4)

CHAPTER 16

　　　　　　　JULIA IS ILL (1)

Iulia erat aegra. cibum non consumebat. calidissima erat. medicus
quem Lucius vocaverat 'febrem habet,' inquit. 'multi cives febres nunc
habent. bonum tamen remedium scio quod filiae tuae dabo.'

medicus multa remedia puellae aegrae dedit. morbus tamen
ingravescebat. Aemilia prope cubile semper sedebat fabulasque filiae　5
narrabat. ubi filia dormiebat, mater tacita sedebat. saepe flebat. Lucius
ad templa deorum festinavit et sacrificia fecit.

Tullum pater ad villam, quam prope mare habebat, miserat. Epimeles
eum non comitabat quod aeger erat. servi eum benigne acceperunt. ille
tamen tristis erat quod soror erat aegra. in servis erat puer Graecus,　10
duodecim annos natus, nomine Phaedrus.

'cur tam tristis es, Tulle?' rogavit Phaedrus.

'tristis sum quod soror mea est aegra. febrem habet.'

'febres periculosae sunt. sed bono es animo! remedium scio quod
contra febres multum valet. mater me id docuit.'　15

'ubi est mater tua?'

'eheu! mortua est. ego tamen illas herbas scio quae remedium
faciunt. si cupis, illud remedium sorori tuae parabo.'

haec verba Tullum delectant. ad vilicum ruit et ei de Phaedri remedio
narrat. vilicus tamen:　20

'quid Phaedrus de remediis scit? in Urbe sunt medici excellentissimi
quos pater tuus ad cubile Iuliae vocavit.' \ Rome.

calidissimus = very hot	tristis = sad
medicus = doctor	bono es animo = cheer up
febris = fever	multum valet = is very good
ingravesco = I get worse	vilicus = bailiff steward
tacitus = silent	

VOCABULARY 16

morbus	= disease	sinister	= left
templum	= temple	dexter	= right
cīvis (cīvis, c)	= citizen	ille	= that, he
hostis (hostis, c)	= enemy	doceō (2)	= I teach
nāvis (nāvis, f)	= ship	petō (3)	= I seek
nūbēs (nūbis, f)	= cloud	rapiō (3½)	= I seize
pars (partis, f)	= part	sciō (4)	= I know
mors (mortis, f)	= death	benignē	= kindly
cubīle (cubīlis, n)	= bed	nunc	= now
mare (maris, n)	= sea	nihil	= nothing

GLADIATORES: GLADIATORS

Just as popular as chariots racing in the Circus were gladiators fighting in the amphitheatre. At first shows were put on at irregular intervals and paid for by private citizens or magistrates seeking popularity. Later the Emperors put on frequent shows to keep the people happy.

The middle part of the amphitheatre was called the HARENA (arena) because it was sprinkled with sand (Latin 'harena') so that the gladiators would not slip in the blood.

Gladiators usually fought in pairs in different parts of the arena simultaneously, each urged on by his instructor (LANISTA). Before the fight began, they saluted the Emperor, if he was presiding, with the words 'AVE, IMPERATOR. MORITURI TE SALUTANT'. ('Hail, Emperor. Those about to die salute you').

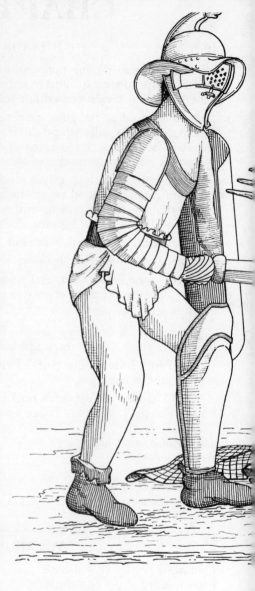

One of the most popular fights was between a RETIARIUS (netman), wearing no armour and carrying a net (RETE) and a three-pronged spear (TRIDENS), and a SECUTOR (chaser), a fully armed swordsman. The odds were about 5 to 3 on the netman winning.

The fight was to the death but if one gladiator was wounded or fallen, the crowd would ask for his release (MISSIO) if he had fought well. They indicated their wishes with their thumbs but it is not certain how. It was not exactly like our thumbs up and thumbs down. After seeing what the crowd wanted the Emperor made a decision and the winning gladiator killed or spared his opponent. The loser was expected not to flinch but to die elegantly. Between contests fresh sand was sprinkled and the bodies were dragged out by attendants dressed as demons of the Underworld. If a body showed signs of life, it was despatched with a mallet.

Gladiators were mainly recruited from criminals, prisoners of war and slaves but sometimes free men volunteered. Like bullfighters in Spain today successful gladiators became immensely rich and popular. When a gladiator had won many victories, he was presented with a wooden sword (RUDIS), which signified honourable retirement.

*Today is the first day of Games put on by the Emperor Domitian. Appius
and Aulus are among the thousands of spectators. They miss Marcus.*

octo gladiatores in variis partibus harenae pugnant. prope Aulum et
Appium secutor Gallus cum retiario Afro pugnat. ille gladium et
scutum, hic rete et tridentem habet.

retiarius circum secutorem saltat et clamat: 'quid times? cur non
pugnas?' ille tamen nihil respondet et in suo loco manet. retiarius rete   5
suum in caput secutoris conicit. ille tamen rete vitat partemque retis
gladio secat. inde retiarius pedes secutoris reti longo petit et pedem
sinistrum capit. ille ad terram cadit. Afer triumphans illum tridente
petit. subito tamen secutor rete rapit et retiarium ad terram trahit.
simul tridentem gladio suo pulsat. tridens per auras volat et in harenam 10
cadit.

Afer agilis celeriter surgit tridentemque suum petit. dextra manu
tridentem rapit, sinistra globum harenae madidae capit. Gallus lente
surgit et pedem suum reti extricat. iterum pugnant. retiarius tamen rete
non iam habet. secutor, ubi hoc videt, 'mortuus es,' clamat. 'cur diutius 15
pugnas? Galli Afros semper vincunt.' his verbis Afrum gladio petit. hic
tamen harenam, quam in manu sinistra habet, in oculos illius subito
conicit. inde, dum Gallus attonitus harenam ex oculis quatit, tridentem
in iugulum illius inmittit. ille ad terram cadit. turba clamat. multi
missionem petunt, multi mortem. tandem tacent et oculos in   20
Imperatorem coniciunt. Imperator missionem dat, sed frustra. Gallus
iam mortuus est.

pars (partis) = part	*volo = I fly*
salto = I dance	*dexter = right*
nihil = nothing	*manu = in the hand*
seco = I cut	*globus = ball*
peto = I go for, look for	*madidus = wet*
sinister = left	*diutius = longer*
rapio = I seize	*quatio = I shake*
simul = at the same time	*iugulum = throat*
pulso = I hit	*mors (mortis) = death*
aura = air	*Imperator = Emperor*

Exercise 16 C

Here are some Third Declension nouns. Decline them in full:—

hostis (hostis, *c*) = enemy.
dens (dentis, *m*) = tooth.
rete (retis, *n*) = net.

Here are some more nouns. Answer the questions below.

mare (maris,*n*) = sea   navis (navis,*f*) = ship
urbs (urbis,*f*) = city   pars (partis,*f*) = part
fames (famis,*f*) = hunger

Give acc. sing. of:—   pars, mare.
Give abl. sing. of:—   fames, mare.
Give abl. plur. of:—   urbs, navis.
Give nom. plur. of:—   pars, navis.
Give gen. plur. of:—   navis, urbs.

Exercise 16 D

1. cives boni in urbe nostra habitant.
2. nomina navium non audivi.
3. hostes mari et terra vincemus.
4. dux hostium per montes fugit.
5. pars fabulae est vera, pars falsa.

Exercise 16 E

1. Clouds cover part of the mountain.
2. Roman citizens have defeated the enemy* by sea.
3. We have captured the leader of the enemy.
4. I had put your clothes on to your bed.
5. We shall attack the city by night.
6. Roman soldiers never fear death.

* *When 'enemy' means 'enemy army', it is usually plural—'hostes'.*

ILLE = THAT (Grammar page 12)

Note:—Ille and Hic are often used in contrast and can be translated:—'that . . this . .'; 'the one . . the other . .'; 'the former . . the latter'.

E.g. (1) hi pueri laborant, illi ludunt.
These boys are working, those are playing.

(2) ille gladium, hic tridentem habebat.
The former had a sword, the latter a trident.

Ille (or hic) sometimes shows that the subject has changed. 'nostri milites impetum magnum in Gallos fecerunt; illi fugerunt'.
= 'Our men made a big attack on the Gauls; they fled.

Exercise 16 F

1. illae naves milites nostros ad Africam portabunt.
2. quis illud dixit?
3. nomen illius fluminis est Tiberis.
4. in illis hortis sunt multae rosae.
5. telum in militem conieci; ille ad terram cecidit.
6. in illa via sunt duodecim tabernae.
7. illi milites muros defenderunt, hi fugerunt.

Exercise 16 G

1. puella parva in cubili parvo dormit.
2. bellum terra marique geremus.
3. in illa urbe multi cives febrem habent.
4. eius villa est in dextra ripa fluminis.
5. remedium bonum scio quod senex me docuit.
6. canis, cui aquam dedisti, mortuus est.

Exercise 16 H

1. They have seized our ships and killed our sailors.
2. The citizens have shut the gates of the city.
3. A large part of the crowd will have left.
4. The king of the island had received the sailors kindly.
5. After dinner my grandfather always used to sleep.
6. Surely you know the names of the consuls?
7. The enemy's chiefs are now seeking peace.
8. Do clouds cover the sea?

PRONOUNS

Pronouns usually refer to someone or something that has already been mentioned. For example in the sentence 'Rufus entered the room; he was carrying a dead cat' the pronoun 'he' refers to 'Rufus'. In the example 'remedium bonum scio quod senex me docuit' 'quod' refers to 'remedium'.

Exercise 16 I Questions about 16 A.

1. To whom or what do these pronouns refer:— ille (9), me (15), id (15), quae (17), ei (19)?
2. In what tense is:— erat (1), vocaverat (2), scio (3), dabo (3), dedit (4)?
3. In what case is:— quem (2), cives (2), febres (2), filiae (3), cubile (5)?
4. What part of speech is:— cibum (1), aegrae (4), prope (5), et (7), ille (9)?

OTHER EXERCISES

Exercise 16 J Questions about 16 B.

1. List in short sentences all the moves and counter-moves of the fight. There are about six main moves and about six counter-moves. The retiarius does most of the attacking. (15)
2. To whom or what do these pronouns refer:- ille (2), hic (3), ille (5), ille (6), quam (17)? (5)
3. How many gladiators (line 1) are fighting in the arena? (1)
4. What weapons do the secutor and retiarius use? (4)
5. What does the retiarius shout at the secutor (4–5)? Why do you think he says these things? (5)
6. What is the secutor's reaction? (2)
7. Who wins the fight? What happens to the loser? (3)

Exercise 16 K Practice at Pronouns.

1. quid mihi dedisti?
2. nobiscum veniet.
3. eam mittam.
4. eius avus est consul.
5. eorum mater venit.
6. hanc epistolam legi.
7. esne puella cuius pater est consul?
8. flumen quod vidimus erat Tiberis.

Exercise 16 L Translate into Latin.—

While I am drinking wine with Marcus in a little inn, a drunken soldier enters.

'I want wine, innkeeper,' he cries.

'Have you money?' asks the innkeeper.

'No,' replies the soldier. 'But tomorrow I shall have money.'

'If you don't have money, you don't drink.'

Marcus however is kind and buys a cup of wine for the soldier. After the soldier has drunk the wine, he turns* to me.

'Surely you'll buy wine for a soldier?'

'No,' I reply. 'You have drunk too-much.'

'I have not drunk too-much. You are insulting me.'

He attacks me but falls to the ground. We carry him out-of the inn and throw him into the river. He swims to the bank with-difficulty. How we laugh!

* *turns = se vertit*

Exercise 16 M

Translate the following Latin sentences as best you can. All the words starting with Z are make-up words to which you may assign any meaning. But you must translate the endings correctly.

Example: 'zincus zundam zillavit' could mean 'The gardener planted a bush' but not 'The gardener will plant a bush' because -avit is a perfect ending. 'zundam' is accusative and must be the object.

1. hostes zellem ceperunt.
2. avus meus zummos zettabit.
3. zenda zopham zagabit.
4. zinci cum zurris zidabant.
5. zonnae filius zuli filiam pulsat.
6. zippos in zappa zandivimus.
7. nonne hoc zostrum zibes?

CHAPTER 17

THE AMPHITHEATRE

The largest and most famous amphitheatre in Rome was the AMPHI-THEATRUM FLAVIUM, named after the family of emperors called the Flavii. The first of these, Vespasian, began it and it was enlarged by his son Titus and opened in A.D. 80. Later it was called the COLOSSEUM because near it was a colossus (large statue) of the Emperor Nero.

It could hold about 45,000 spectators. Although the shows were free, tickets were required for entry. There were seventy-six doors and inside was an elaborate system of stairways and passages so that spectators could reach their seats easily. The Emperor and those with him had a special box, the front rows were reserved for senators, the next fourteen rows for knights. Then came the main area for other citizens, and higher and further back were rough benches for foreigners, slaves and the like. Women had to watch from an open gallery at the top. Higher still were masts to support awnings which gave protection against the sun.

A fifteen foot wall with rollers and overhanging mesh prevented the beasts from jumping into the audience. The floor of the arena was wood, sprinkled with sand. Beneath it were numerous dens for beasts, and lifts to bring up elaborate scenery.

Besides gladiatorial fights there were VENATIONES (hunts). In these either beasts fought beasts or beasts were killed by BESTIARII (beast fighters) or beasts killed criminals.

Often elaborate scenery was quickly assembled (woods, islands, hills) and famous stories were acted with characters really dying. For example Icarus might plunge to his death trying to fly or Actaeon be torn to pieces by hounds.

Occasionally the arena was flooded or a lake was used and NAUMACHIAE (seafights) were held. The boats were manned by condemned criminals who had been promised that, if they fought well, the survivors would be pardoned.

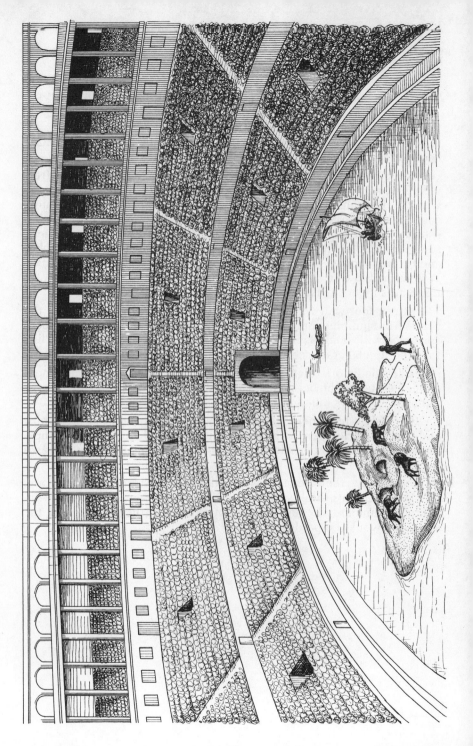

Today is the fourth day of the Games. Aulus and Appius are there again.
They have already watched the slaughter of an amazing number of beasts.
Now an island with trees and caves is being quickly built in the arena. What
will the next entertainment be?

magister ludorum harenam intravit et 'nunc', inquit 'cantor Graecus
vobis cantabit. nos—
(fremitus et gemitus)
—nos Romani non sumus barbari. Romanos non solum artes belli sed
etiam artes pacis delectant. nonne iam satis pugnarum vidistis? nonne   5
carmen cupitis?
(fremitus et gemitus)
nunc igitur Glyceraides de morte Orphei cantabit. Orpheus erat cantor
ille Graecus cuius carmina etiam saevas bestias mulcebant.'

in harena servi insulam aedificaverant et in insula montem. in monte   10
erant multae cavernae. e dextra caverna venit Glyceraides, cantor
Graecus. vestes Graecas et lyram gerebat. voce magna cantavit. pauci
tamen carmen eius audiebant.

aquam interea servi in harenam inmittebant. iam aqua erat duo
pedes alta. iam scapha virginum pulchrarum plena per aquam lente   15
procedebat. virgines cantabant floresque ad cantorem coniciebant.

magister ludorum signum dedit. iam crocodilos et hippopotamos
servi in aquam inmiserunt. turba tacuit. Glyceraides, hoc silentio
laetus, voce magna cantavit. virgines vocibus teneris cantaverunt. iam
scapha ad insulam appropinquabat.   20

subito e cavernis bestiae veniebant, ursae et leones et pantherae
nigrae. primo cantor bestias non vidit. spectatores riserunt. inde
panthera in saxo prope eum sedit. spectatores iterum riserunt. subito
pantheram vidit. attonitus circumspectavit. ceteras bestias vidit.
territus fugit. dum tamen pantheram vitat, in ursam ruit.   25

unus e spectatoribus 'cur fugis?' clamavit. 'cur bestias carmine tuo
non mulces? Orpheus enim es.' tota turba risit. virgines quoque, quae
erant in scapha, riserunt. Glyceraides non risit. mortuus erat.

ludus = game	mulceo = I soothe
cantor = singer	aedifico = I build
fremitus et gemitus = growls and	mons (montis) = mountain
groans	lyra = lyre
solum = only	paucus = few
ars (artis) = art	altus = high, deep
etiam = also, even	scapha = boat
saevus = savage	virgo (virginis) = maiden
bestia = beast	flos (floris) = flower

Glyceraides mortuus erat. corpus duo leones consumebant. spectaculum turbam iam magnopere delectabat.

magister ludorum signum iterum dedit. subito virgines clamores terribiles dabant. scapha submergebatur. servus qui hoc fecerat e scapha fugit et ad murum celeriter natavit. crocodilos vitavit. tres e 5 virginibus in aquam desiluerunt et ad murum natabant. crocodilos non vitaverunt. duae virginum ad insulam fugerunt. hae cibum non crocodilis sed leonibus praebebant. una virgo in scapha mansit, sed frustra. hippopotamus iratus scapham magna vi submersit virginemque dentibus necavit. spectatores ridebant et plaudebant. 10

'quanta iactura!' clamavit Aulus. 'quis tam pulchras puellas morte condemnavit?'

Appius 'iure' inquit 'iudices eas condemnaverunt. duae enim fuerunt veneficae. dominum suum venenaverunt. ceterae erant Iudaeae aut Christianae, hostes populi Romani, quae deos nostros non colunt.' 15

'quis Glyceraidem condemnavit?'

'vox Glyceraidis Glyceraidem condemnavit. cantor malus est, immo fuit. carmina eius Imperatorem vexabant. Imperator tamen iram celavit et Glyceraidi 'cantor bonus es,' inquit. 'nonne populo cantabis? populum Romanum non solum artes belli sed etiam artes pacis 20 delectant. satis pugnarum viderunt. carmina tua eos delectabunt.' Glyceraides igitur cantavit. cantoris mors erat Imperatoris iocus.'

clamor = shout, cry	iure = rightly
submergebatur = was sinking	iudex (iudicis) = judge
desilio = I jump down	veneficus = poisoner
praebeo = I provide	Iudaeus = Jew
vis = force	aut = or
dens (dentis) = tooth	colo = I worship
plaudo = I applaud	immo = or rather
quanta iactura = What a waste	iocus = joke

VOCABULARY 17

iūdex (iūdicis, C)	= judge	vis (F) = { force strength	
virgō (virginis, F)	= maiden		
imperātor (imperātōris, M)	= general	saevus	= savage
Imperātor	= Emperor	paucus	= few
clāmor (clāmōris, M)	= shout	altus	= high, deep
flōs (flōris, M)	= flower	aut	= either, or
mons (montis, M)	= mountain	sōlum	= only
dens (dentis, M)	= tooth	etiam	= also, even
ars (artis, F)	= art	enim	= for
Iuppiter (Iovis, M)	= Jupiter		
aedificō (1)	= I build		

SUM

In this chapter you meet all the tenses of Sum. See page 29 in the Grammar.

When translating into Latin, NOTE:

(1) When the verb is Sum, there is a subject but no object. E.g. in the sentence 'The boy is mad.' both 'boy' and 'mad' are in the nominative.

(2) In the sentence 'There are wolves in the wood.' the word 'there' is not translated. The sentence becomes 'Wolves are in the wood.'

Exercise 17 C

1. fuisti.
2. fuerit.
3. eratis.
4. fuerant.
5. fuerunt.
6. We have been.
7. We shall be.
8. He had been.
9. I have been.
10. You will have been.

Exercise 17 D

1. The ditches are full.
2. They have been friends.
3. You are tired, Aulus.
4. You are tired, sailors.
5. We shall be alone.
6. There are deep rivers.
7. You are Roman citizens.
8. Once he had been king.
9. She is my mother.
10. There will be a big dinner.

Exercise 17 E

1. When shall we see our sons and daughters again?
2. The guards had defended the gate with great courage.
3. Afterwards a lion dragged the body into a ditch.
4. Is the river deep? Are there many enemy?
5. We have always been friends. Why do you abandon a friend?
6. They have slain not only the Emperor but also the consuls.

APPOSITION

A noun added to another noun to describe it further is said to be in apposition to it. It agrees with the first noun in case.

Example: Marcum, fratrem tuum, vidi.

Exercise 17 F

1. muros oppidi magna vi oppugnabamus.
2. senem horribilem vidi qui barbam habebat.
3. iter longum per montes faciemus.
4. hostes aut in montes aut in silvas fugerint.
5. si puer bonus fueris, fabulam tibi narrabo.
6. avus vester vires hippopotami habet.
7. Iuliamne, sororem meam, vidisti?
8. milites itinere longo fessi mox dormiverunt.
9. Lucius equum Marco, filio suo, dederat.
10. Aesculapius erat filius Apollinis. Apollo erat filius Iovis, regis deorum.

Exercise 17 G (Apposition)

Before translating each sentence think to which word the words underlined refer and therefore in what case they will be.

1. I have not seen Titus, <u>the Emperor</u>.
2. Not far from Britain is Mona, <u>a small island</u>.
3. I was sitting with Quartus, <u>a foolish old-man</u>.
4. We shall defeat the Scots, <u>our enemies</u>.
5. <u>My friend</u> Aulus' dog is dead.

OTHER EXERCISES

Exercise 17 H Questions about 17 A.

1. In the first twelve lines find Latin words from which these English
   words are derived: arena, mortal, videotape, insulate, pugnacious.
2. In what tense is:— intravit (1), cantabit (2), sumus (4), vidistis (5),
   mulcebant (9)?
3. In what case is:— ludorum (1), vobis (2), artes (5) carmen (6), morte
   (8)?
4. What part of speech is:— harenam (1), nos (4), non (4), sed (4), saevas
   (9)?

Exercise 17 I Questions about 17 A and 17 B.

1. Who was Orpheus?
2. How had Glyceraides angered the Emperor?
3. Why did Glyceraides want to sing in the arena?
4. Did the spectators like Glyceraides as a change from gladiators?
5. Why did they fall silent (line 18)?
6. What is the point of the spectator's remarks in lines 26 and 27?
7. Who caused the boat to sink? How do you think it was done?
8. Why had the girls been condemned to death?
9. Do you think the attitude of Aulus and Appius is heartless? Can you
   think of similar people today? Write some things they might say.
10. What is the spectators' attitude? Can you think of similar people
    today?

Exercise 17 J Vocabulary Practice.

1. sagittae longae.
2. saxa alta.
3. timores stulti.
4. verba tenera.
5. vires magnae.
6. feminae territae.
7. arma nova.
8. iudices mali.
9. carmina pulchra.
10. ceteri senes.

Exercise 17 K Questions about 17 A, lines 21–28.

1. What beasts come out of the caves?   (3)
2. Why did the spectators laugh (line 22)   (2)
3. Why did the spectators laugh again (23)?   (2)
4. Explain why the singer was astonished (24).   (3)
5. Explain fully why the spectators laughed (26–27).   (5)

Exercise 17 L

There are about a dozen mistakes in the following story. See if you can find them and in each case say what the correct word or phrase should be.

A DAY AT THE RACES

Today Tullus has been invited by his friend Titus to go to the chariot races. Their grammaticus has given them leave of absence from school. Tullus is up before dawn and after a quick prandium is taken by Epimeles, his tutor, to Titus' house. From there Titus' father takes them to the Amphitheatrum Flavium where the races are held. They have very good seats as Titus' father is a senator. He is wearing his toga laticlavia and Titus and Tullus each wears a smart toga praetexta.

The place is very full, packed with nearly 400,000 spectators. Now the four teams are led into the carceres by their lanistae. Now the Emperor Domitian drops the alba linea and they are off. Over the sand they race and round the meta.

'Prasini! Prasini!' cries Tullus.

'Nigri! Nigri!' cries Titus.

Down the second straight close to the spina the chariots speed and round the meta. The Greens are ahead. One lap completed, then two, then three. Tullus watches the dolphins and counts. But now he is in for a bitter disappointment. At the next corner the Green auriga grazes his right wheel on one of the four conical pillars at the meta. The chariot tips over, the driver is thrown to the ground and the Greens are out of the race.

However, Tullus cheers up when Greens win the next two races and then it is time for the picnic. Cold roast chickens, fresh bread, black olives, green olives, lettuce, tomatoes, little honey cakes, apples, cherries and finally snow-cooled black coffee. Tullus tucks in.

CHAPTER 18

ROMAN MEDICINE

When ancient doctors prescribed medicines, they were largely working in the dark. In the first place it was difficult to know whether the medicine worked or not. Most patients recover anyway and others improve because they *think* the medicine is doing them good. Secondly the ancient doctor did not really know what effect the disease had on the patient nor what effect the drug had. However, trial and error gradually built up a body of knowledge. If a certain medicine had worked once, it would probably work again.

Some ancient medicines correspond to modern ones. Juice of poppy seeds was given to crying babies and today morphine, made from poppies, is used to relieve pain. Juice of autumn crocus was used to relieve gout and it is still so used today. Extract of bark of willow (salix, salicis) was used to reduce fever, and aspirin, made from salicylic acid, is used for this purpose today, though it is usually now made from coal and not from willow bark.

Most medicines, however, were useless. For example an Egyptian recipe for baldness was: 'Fat of lion, fat of hippopotamus, fat of crocodile, fat of cat, fat of serpent, fat of ibex, smeared on the head.'

Since it was not usually known which ingredient produced the beneficial effect, medicines often included ten or twenty, most of which were useless and some disgusting. In fact strong-smelling medicines sold well. 'If it smells as horrible as this, it *must* be good for me,' said the patient. Similarly, expensive medicines such as pearls dissolved in wine sold well. 'If it costs as much as this, it *must* be good,' said the patient.

Poisons also had many ingredients, since it was not known which ones actually did the poisoning. These could not be obtained from doctors but were sold by wicked hags, who also supplied love philtres, which were drugs supposed to make a person fall in love with you. Love philtres never worked but many hoped they would and bought them.

Many people in the ancient world believed that the gods had healing powers. In particular Aesculapius, son of Apollo, once a mortal doctor, was worshipped as the god of healing. An essential part of the treatment was to spend the night in his temple. In Rome this was on the Insula Tiberina in the river Tiber. An island was obviously a good place to isolate infectious diseases and there is still a hospital there today.

Each Roman fort had its hospital, Valetudinarium, and later hospitals were built for civilians. Of ancient doctors the most famous is the Greek Hippocrates who practised on the island of Cos. The Hippocratic Oath, which contains all the things that a doctor must and must not do, is still sworn today in a modified form by those entering the medical profession.

JULIA IS ILL (2)

Can you remember these words from 16 A:—medicus, febris, vilicus, multum valet, morbus ingravescit?

Tullus erat tristis. nuntium tristem acceperat. servus, quem pater ad villam cotidie mittebat, haec verba dixerat:

'Iulia infirmior est. morbus ingravescit. difficile est medicis tam gravem morbum sanare.'

Tullus ad vilicum cucurrit. 5

'Iuliae morbus ingravescit,' clamat. 'remedium Phaedri temptare debemus. ad Urbem statim festinare debemus remedium Iuliae datum.'

vilicus dubitavit.

'quid pueri,' inquit 'de remediis sciunt? si Phaedri remedium Iuliam non sanaverit, pater tuus iratus erit.' 10

'iratus erit si de Phaedri remedio post Iuliae mortem audiverit.'

haec verba vilicum moverunt.

'quod dicis,' inquit 'verum est. Phaedrum ad Urbem hodie mittam.'

'ego cum eo iter facere debeo. nam si pater Phaedrum non audiverit, fortasse me audiet.' 15

'te ad Urbem non mittam. multi cives febres habent. si te ad Urbem misero, pater tuus iratus erit.'

'iratus erit, si de vino quod bibis audiverit. saepe ebrius es.'

vilicus timebat.

'o Tulle, quod dicis non verum est. numquam ebrius sum. multum 20 vini bibo quod vinum contra febres multum valet. si tamen cum Phaedro iter facere adeo cupis, te mittam.'

Tullus, ubi hoc audivit, vilicum complexus 'euge!' clamat. 'Iuliam servavisti! sed statim discedere debemus.'

nuntius = message	*dubito = I hestitate*
tristis = sad	*quod (REMEMBER) = what OR*
infirmior = weaker	*because*
difficilis = difficult	*adeo = so*
gravis = serious	*complexus = hugging.*
sano = I heal, cure	*Euge! = Hurray!*
tempto = I try	
debeo = I ought	

JULIA IS ILL (3)

Iulia infirmior erat. parentes desperabant. Lucius templum Aesculapii petivit et deo sacrificium fecit. sacerdos Lucio 'sacrificium,' inquit 'non satis est. necesse est filiae tuae unam noctem in hoc templo dormire.'

'filia mea,' respondit Lucius 'paene mortua est. periculosum erit eam per vias portare.' 5

'deus Aesculapius eam servabit. facile erit eam per urbem nocte portare, ubi pauci homines sunt in viis.'

'quod mones faciam. si Aesculapius filiam meam servaverit, candelabrum aureum in hoc templo ponam.'

Aemilia, ubi Lucius verba sacerdotis ei narravit, 'hoc consilium,' 10
inquit 'insanum est. periculosum erit puellam aegram per vias urbis nocte portare et in templo frigido relinquere, nec tamen necesse est. hodie Tullus a villa cum servo Phaedro revenit. Phaedrus remedium bonum scit quod contra febres multum valet. mater eum id docuit.'

'quid puer de remediis scit? quid servus? fortasse mater eius fuit 15
venefica. hoc remedium timeo.'

Aemilia tamen 'ego,' inquit 'puero credo. Tullus quoque credit. Tullum et servum vocabo.'

Tullus et Phaedrus intrant. Tullus ad patrem currit et 'pater, pater,' clamat. 'ecce Phaedrus qui Iuliam servabit. remedium bonum scit.' 20

Lucius servo 'quas herbas,' inquit 'petere necesse est hoc medicamentum paratum?'

Phaedrus 'necesse est,' respondit 'librum salicis in aqua coquere.'

diu pater cogitavit. inde: 'hoc remedium est simplex et purum nec difficile erit id parare. ad flumen statim festinare debes salices petitum.' 25

'medicamentum iam feci.'

'bene fecisti. ambo remedia temptabimus. Iulia et medicamentum Phaedri bibet et unam noctem in templo Aesculapii dormiet.'

quod constituerunt faciunt. Iulia medicamentum quod Phaedrus fecit bibit. non unam sed tres noctes in templo Aesculapii dormit. lente 30
febris eam relinquit. lente Iulia convalescit.

quam laeti sunt parentes!

Aemilia 'o Luci,' clamat 'quam bonum fuit consilium tuum! quam recte Aesculapio credidisti! timores mei fuerunt stulti. deus filiam nostram servavit. donum magnum deo dare debemus.' 35

Lucius 'o Aemilia,' clamat 'quam bonum fuit consilium tuum! quam recte Phaedro credidisti! timores mei fuerunt stulti. Phaedri remedium filiam nostram servavit. candelabrum aureum deo dabo, Phaedro libertatem.'

sacerdos (sacerdotis) = priest	*librum salicis = bark of willow*
facilis = easy	*coquo = I cook, boil*
candelabrum aureum = golden	*cogito = I think*
lampstand	*bene = well*
consilium = idea, plan	*ambo = both*
nec = nor, and not	*et .. et .. = both .. and ...*
venefica = poisoner, witch	*constituo = I decide*
credo = I trust, believe (in)	*recte = rightly*
	libertas (libertatis) = freedom.

VOCABULARY 18

cōnsilium	= plan	ācer	= keen, fierce
nūntius	= ⌠messenger	trīstis	= sad
	⌡message	omnis	= all
lībertās	= freedom	gravis	= ⌠heavy
(lībertātis, F) ⌡			⌡serious
sanguis	⌡= blood	turpis	= disgraceful
(sanguinis, M)		facilis	= easy
dubitō (1)	⌠= I doubt	difficilis	= difficult
	⌡ I hesitate	fortis	= brave
vulnerō (1)	= I wound	brevis	= short
dēbeō (2)	= I ought, owe	nec	= nor, and not
cōnstituō (3)	= I decide	nec . . nec . .	= neither . . nor
et . . et . .	= both . . and . .		

ADJECTIVES CONTINUED

In this chapter you learn Acer and Tristis and other adjectives which decline like them. They can be found on page 8 in the Grammar.

Exercise 18 C

Make acer agree with:— militem, puerum, duces, Gallos, hostium.
Make tristis agree with:— belli, fabulas, fratribus, carmen, epistolam.
Make omnis agree with: agros, flumina, cibum, civibus, armorum.

Exercise 18 D

1. milites nostri sunt fortes et acres.
2. hostes omnia oppida ceperant.
3. carmina tristia numquam cantamus.
4. nonne hoc consilium turpe est?
5. omnium militum onera sunt gravia.
6. in Galliam via facili iter fecimus.

Exercise 18 E

1. Brave boys do not cry, Tullus.
2. All the tasks are difficult.
3. You are carrying a heavy burden.
4. The Emperor gave gifts to all the soldiers.
5. We are fighting against fierce enemies.
6. Your letters are always short.

THE INFINITIVE

Infinitives are the parts of the verb which start with the word 'TO'. E.g. 'To love', 'To be heard.' The Present Infinitive is the second Principal Part:—

AMARE = TO LOVE   MONERE = TO ADVISE   REGERE = TO RULE

CAPERE = TO TAKE   AUDIRE = TO HEAR   ESSE = TO BE

THE SUPINE

The Supine is the last Principal Part and means 'In order to . . .' E.g. auditum = in order to hear.

Exercise 18 F

Give the present infinitive of: navigo, facio, duco, aperio, timeo, do, fleo.
And the supine of:— dormio, paro, rapio.

Exercise 18 G

1. fugere est turpe.
2. turpe est fugere.
3. turpe est militibus Romanis fugere.
4. facile erit hoc oppidum capere.
5. difficile erat medico tam gravem morbum sanare.
6. Lucius filiam in templo relinquere constituit.
7. libertatem huic servo dare debemus.
8. pueros in cubicula sua dormitum misi.
9. hic mercator ad Britanniam navigare parat.
10. in forum consulem auditum festinavimus.
11. flumen intrare milites nostri non dubitaverunt.

Exercise 18 H

1. I have decided to inspect the gardens today.
2. The enemy did not hesitate to enter the water.
3. We ought to send help immediately.
4. It is difficult to read your letters.
5. It is disgraceful to laugh (at) your grandfather.
6. It will be easy for brave soldiers to defeat the enemy.

OTHER EXERCISES

Exercise 18 I. Questions about 18 B

1. Give an English word derived from:— satis (3), unam (3), noctem (3), dormire (3), urbem (6).
2. In what tense is:— desperabant (1), fecit (2), est (3), servabit (6), servaverit (8)?
3. In what case is:— templum (1), deo (2), Lucio (2), nocte (6), viis (7)?
4. What part of speech is:— infirmior (1), fecit (2), non (2), in (3), eam (4)?

Exercise 18 J More questions about 18 A & B.

1. What god was Aesculapius? Where was his temple in Rome?
2. What gift did Lucius promise to the god if Julia recovered?
3. Why was Aemilia at first against entrusting her daughter to Aesculapius?
4. Why was Lucius at first against Phaedrus' remedy?
5. What was Phaedrus' medicine made from?
6. Who or what do you think eventually cured Julia?
7. What was Phaedrus' reward?
8. What do we learn in this story (all three passages) about the character of Tullus?
9. What do we learn in this story (all passages) about the characters of Lucius and Aemilia?

Exercise 18 K Verb Practice.

1. vestes emebant.
2. urbem relinquam.
3. caput suum texit.
4. discedimus.
5. quid dixisti?

6. He has departed.
7. They were playing.
8. What have you bought?
9. They will flee.
10. She is standing.

Exercise 18 L Translate into Latin

Yesterday I was fighting against a Gallic secutor by name Holcus. He tried to make me angry.

'Why are you afraid?' he shouted. 'Why are you avoiding me?'

I didn't reply but suddenly cast my net and caught his left foot. I ran forward in-order-to-thrust my spear into his throat but suddenly fell to the ground. I got-up immediately and looked-for my spear and net. My net was near Holcus. I was in great danger. I picked up my spear and a ball of wet sand. We Africans are cunning. When Holcus came-at me, I threw the sand into his eyes. Then I launched my spear at his throat.

Exercise 18 M. Mixed Pronouns

1. quis hoc fecit?
2. id mihi dedit.
3. tecum veniam.
4. quid ei debes?
5. ex illo oppido fugerunt.
6. ego et tu eos vincemus.
7. quis illud tibi dixit?
8. eius filius revenit.
9. puellae quas vidimus erant consulis filiae.
10. librum quem mihi dedisti saepe lego.

Exercise 18 N. Odd Man Out.

1. gladius, pugio, <u>pilum</u>, tridens. *[thrown not held.]*
2. <u>gladius</u>, galea, lorica, scutum. *[only weapon, others defensive.]*
3. nuntius, <u>opus</u>, avus, populus. *[neuter others M.]*
4. Iuppiter, Charon, <u>Styx</u>, Aesculapius. *[Styx is a river]*
5. facilis, <u>salicis</u>, brevis, fortis. *[? noun]*
6. oleum, palaestra, <u>vitrum</u>, piscina. *[indoors]*
7. tempora, corpora, <u>carmina</u>, insula. *[sing. others pl.]*

Exercise 18 O Questions about 18 B, lines 1–9.

1. What was Julia's condition (1)? How did her parents feel? (2)
2. What did Lucius do? Who was Aesculapius? (3)
3. What did the priest say (2–3)? (3)
4. Why did Lucius not like the idea (4–5)? (2)
5. What two things did the priest say to persuade him (6–7)? (2)
6. Which words tell you that Lucius was persuaded? (1)
7. What did he offer, if his daughter were cured? (2)

CHAPTER 19

LETTERS IN ROMAN TIMES

For short letters, that did not have to go far, wax tablets called codicilli or pugillares were used. For longer letters the writer wrote with ink on papyrus, a rough paper made from papyrus reeds. The ink was made from a mixture of soot, gum and water. The pen was made from a reed or goosefeather, which from time to time had to be sharpened with a penknife.

Personal letters were written in the writer's own hand; otherwise he dictated to secretaries. The pages were pasted together, rolled up, tied with thread and sealed with wax and a signet ring. On the outside was written the name and rough address of the person to whom the letter was to be delivered.

There was no postal service for private citizens. The Imperial Post was very efficient but was for official business only. There were posting houses at convenient distances where the messengers could change horses. They averaged fifty miles a day but went faster if the message was urgent.

For private citizens there were three methods of sending letters. Firstly you could send a slave (servus tabellarius). Secondly you could ask friends or strangers who were going to the right destination to deliver your letters. It was not thought to be unreasonable to ask chance acquaintances to do this. In return you might give them letters of introduction to people. Thirdly, if you were influential enough, you might use the tax-gatherers' couriers (publicanorum tabellarii). Tabellarii covered about twenty six miles a day on foot and fifty in vehicles. A letter from Britain to Rome took about thirty-three days.

A letter opened with a greeting such as: "Marcus Quinto S.D.P." (Salutem dicit plurimam). The phrase was used both to acquaintances and close relations so may be translated "Marcus sends his greetings to Quintus" or "Marcus sends his love to Quintus." Later in the letter there might occur the phrase "Terentia impertit tibi salutem" (Terentia sends you her love) or "Salutem Terentiae dices" (Will you give my love to Terentia"). The first sentence of the letter was often "Si vales, bene est" (If you are well, that is well) but this phrase was considered rather old-fashioned. "Cura ut valeas" (See that you keep well) was another much used phrase. The letter ended with the one word "Vale" (Farewell).

Aemilia in peristylio cum Tullo et Iulia sedebat. subito Lucius intravit. ridebat et duas epistolas in manu tenebat. cum eo erat tribunus iuvenis.

'ecce Marcus Curtius Postumus qui Marci epistolas e Gallia portavit. alius tribunus eas ei dedit.'

tribuno Aemilia 'quam laetos,' inquit 'nos fecisti.'   5

'vinum tribuno!' clamavit Lucius. servus tribuno vinum dedit. 'dum Postumus vinum bibit, epistolas vobis legam.'

epistola prima

MARCUS PATRI S.D.P.

si vales, bene est. ego valeo. tandem in Britanniam veni! e portu 10 Gesoriaco in portum Dubrim navigavimus. mare, dis gratia, erat tranquillum. viae huius portus sunt angustae et sordidae, tabernae parvae et frigidae. solem numquam videmus, semper nubes!

epistolam a te nondum accepi. num excidit in via? num tabellarii tam neglegentes sunt? haec est quarta quam ad te scripsi. aliasne accepisti? 15 hanc Gaio Titurio tribuno, qui ad Galliam hodie navigat, dabo. brevis igitur est.

salutem plurimam matri dices et Iuliae et Tullo et omnibus. convaluitne Iulia? vale.

manus (4) = hand.	*sol = sun.*
teneo = I hold.	*nondum = not yet.*
alius = (an)other.	*num = surely . . not.*
portus (4) = port.	*excidit = been dropped.*
dis gratia = thanks to the gods.	*convalesco = I get better.*
angustus = narrow.	

epistola secunda

MARCUS PATRI S.D.P.

epistolas tuas tandem accepi. quam laetus sum quod Iulia iam convaluit et quod tu et mater et Tullus febrem omnes vitavistis.

e portu Dubri ad flumen Tamesim iter celeriter fecimus. in ripa 5 fluminis est urbs magna, nomine Londinium. ibi duas noctes mansimus. inde Lindum, inde Eboracum. via est longa sed bona. tempestas frigida. Eboracum est castra magna. ad exercitum tamen Agricolae nondum venimus. nam Agricola cum exercitu contra Caledonios bellum gerit.   10

tempestas = weather	*exercitus(4) = army*
castra = camp	

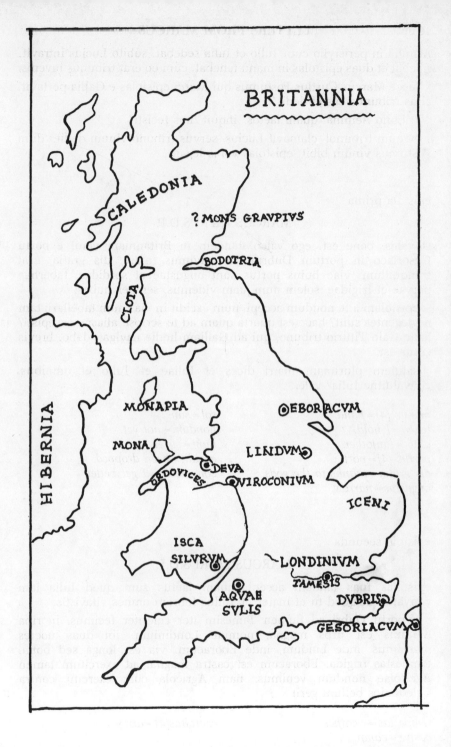

BRITANNIA

CALEDONIA

? MONS GRAVPIVS

BODOTRIA

CLOTA

HIBERNIA

MONAPIA

MONA

ORDOVICES

DEVA

VIROCONIVM

EBORACVM

LINDVM

ICENI

ISCA
SILVRVM

LONDINIVM

TAMESIS

AQVAE
SVLIS

DVBRIS

GESORIACVM

vulnus non grave in genu sinistro accepi. dum in itinere sumus, ego
et duo amici ceteros reliquimus et in silvas venatum equitavimus.
subito barbari in nos impetum faciunt. quod tam pauci sumus, non
pugnamus. dum fugimus, sagitta genu meum vulnerat, dis gratia, non
venenata. convalesco. vale.   15

vulnus (vulneris) = wound	*hunting*
genu(4) = knee	*impetus(4) = attack*
venatum (supine) = in order to hunt,	*venenatus = poisoned.*

ROMAN AQUEDUCTS

The Romans are famous for their aqueducts. Often these ran along the
ground as covered channels. If the ground was uneven, three methods
were used: (1) tunnels; (2) inverted siphons, lead pipes bedded in
concrete; (3) channels carried on arches. These last are the most
spectacular and well-known. The cost was high and was borne by the
town supplied.

As the population of Rome grew, water had to be brought from further
and further away. Eventually there were eleven aqueducts bringing 350
million gallons to Rome daily. The water went to large tanks and from
them by lead pipes to baths, public fountains and private consumers.

Aqueducts were usually named after the magistrates who had
arranged for their construction. For example the first aqueduct, the Aqua
Appia (312 B.C.) was named after Appius Claudius. The Aqua Virgo,
however, a stream of water which was brought to Rome by Marcus
Vipsanius Agrippa, was so named because a young maiden (virgo)
discovered its source.

Aqueducts often leaked, as was noticeable when they passed over
streets.

19 B   **THE DEATH OF DECIUS**

Aemilia sola sedebat. subito Tullus in tablinum ruit.

TUL   mater! mater! audivistine?
MAT   quid dicis?
TUL   nonne de Decio audivisti?
MAT   quid de Decio?   5
TUL   mortuus est!
MAT   quomodo mortuus?
TUL   iugulatus.
MAT   num hoc verum est? quis eum iugulavit?
TUL   Aqua—   10
MAT   aqua? natabatne?
TUL   Virgo—
MAT   virgo? num virgo Decium iugulavit?

iugulatus = throat cut, murdered   *iugulo = I cut the throat, murder.*

55

TUL   minime. Aqua Virgo. Aqua Virgo quae est aquaeductus.
MAT   quid dicis? num insanus es?   15
TUL   minime. heri Decius et Publius ad Porticum Vipsaniam
       ambulabant. dum per portam, quae sub Aqua Virgine est,
       procedunt, multas et longas stirias de porta pendentes vident.
       stant et spectant. subito stiria magna cadit iugulumque Decii
       transfigit. sanguis passim fluit. Publius est territus. 'subvenite! 20
       subvenite!' clamat. nemo tamen est in via. in aliam viam currit.
       nemo in illa via est. in tertiam ruit et duos milites invenit quos
       ad locum ducit. corpus inspiciunt. puer est mortuus.
       'ubi est telum?' rogat miles.
       'stiria eum necavit,' respondet Publius.   25
       'num verum dicis? stiriam non video.'
       ubi est stiria? Publius diligenter quaerit et stiriam minimam in
       vulnere invenit.
       'nunc intellego,' inquit. 'stiria in sanguine calido tabuit.'
       milites stulti Publio non crediderunt. sed verum est, mater! stiria 30
       Decium necavit.
MAT   o miserum Decium! o Mors, ubi non es, si etiam aqua homines
       iugulat?

heri = yesterday.   *subvenite! = Help!*
porticus = portico.   *minimus = very small*
stiria = icicle   *calidus = hot*
pendentes = hanging   *tabeo = I melt*
iugulum = throat   *credo = I believe (in).*
passim = everywhere

VOCABULARY 19

castra (2,N,plur.)	= camp	sōl (sōlis, M)	= sun
vulnus (vulneris, N)	= wound	gradus (4)	= step
tempestās (tempestātis, F) }	= { weather / storm	manus (4, F)	= hand
		portus (4)	= port
alius	= (an)other	impetus (4)	= attack
heri	= yesterday	exercitus (4)	= army
num	= surely not	genū (4, N)	= knee
cōnsilium capiō	= I adopt a plan	teneō (2)	= I hold

QUESTIONS—NUM

In Chapter 3 you met -ne, which asks straightforward questions, e.g. timesne? = Are you afraid?

In Chapter 9 you met Nonne, which asks questions expecting the answer 'Yes', e.g. nonne me times? = Aren't you afraid of me?

Num asks questions which expect the answer 'No':
e.g.   num canem times?
       = Surely you're not afraid of the dog?
       Are you afraid of the dog?
       You're not afraid of the dog, are you?

Exercise 19 C

1. num venis?
2. nonne venis?
3. venisne?
4. num equum times?
5. nonne equum times?

6. Surely you're not going?
7. Surely you knew?
8. Have you heard the song?
9. Surely he's not fled?
10. Hasn't he slept?

THE FOURTH DECLENSION

In this chapter you meet Fourth Declension nouns like GRADUS and GENU. See page 6 of the Grammar.
All nouns like Genu are neuter. Almost all like Gradus are masculine but a few such as MANUS (= hand) are feminine.

Exercise 19 D

1. duo senes in gradibus templi sedebant.
2. impetus multos in nos fecerunt.
3. quod tempestas erat magna, e portu non navigavit.
4. vulnera et in capite et in manu et in genu accepi.
5. necesse est tibi exercitum in castra ducere.
6. num dubitas? impetum statim facere debemus.
7. nonne hoc consilium capies?
8. num hunc iuvenem quaestorem creabitis?

Exercise 19 E

1. Agricola is leader of our army.
2. Your knees are dirty, Tullus.
3. There are few harbours in the island.
4. The Briton held a big sword in his hand.
5. Surely Romans do not fear Britons?
6. Surely they haven't finished the task already?
7. Surely it is disgraceful for a soldier to flee?
8. She touched Marcus' knee with her tender hand.
9. It will not be easy to adopt the plan.
10. The dogs will drink the blood of our enemies.

OTHER EXERCISES

Exercise 19 F   Questions about 19 A.

1. Give nom. sing. of:—Britanniam (10), portu (10), solem (13), nubes (13), tribuno (16).
2. Give abl. sing. of:— mare (11), viae (12), portus (12), solem (13), matri (18).
3. Give nom. sing. masc. of:—huius (12), quam (15), angustae (12), omnibus (18).
4. Give 1st. sing. pres. tense of:—veni (10), accepi (14), scripsi (15).
5. Give present infinitive of:—vales (10), navigavimus (11), erat (11).

Exercise 19 G   More about 19 A. Answer in Latin.

1. quis Marci epistolas ad Lucium portavit?
2. e quo portu Marcus ad Britanniam navigavit?
3. quot noctes Marcus in urbe Londinio mansit?
4. cur Marcus et amici in silvas equitaverunt?
5. cur Marcus et amici cum barbaris non pugnaverunt?

Exercise 19 H   More Practice.

1. Savage dogs have wounded the messenger.
2. Surely you do not fear the dangers of war?
3. Do you see the temple of Jupiter?
4. We had made a long journey through the mountains.
5. Surely it is bad to give money to a judge?
6. We are fighting against fierce enemies.
7. We were tired from the long journey.
8. With his left hand he was holding a shield.

Exercise 19 I   Vocabulary Revision.

1. cenam parare.
2. arma rapere.
3. iram celare.
4. nihil intellegere.
5. consulem creare.
6. consilium capere.
7. diu dubitare.
8. castra defendere.
9. libros legere.
10. exercitum inspicere.

Exercise 19 J   Adjectives.

Make 'magnus' agree with:— vim, itinera, sene, Iovis, domine, capita, exercituum, civi, gradu, virtutem.

Exercise 19 K   Derivations.

Say from what Latin words the following English words are derived. Write sentences (in English) to show that you know the meanings of the English words.

Illegible, senile, invincible, fugitive, culpable, tractor, circumnavigate, invisible, decapitate, subterranean.

Exercise 19 L   Questions about 19 B, lines 16–29.

1. To where were Decius and Publius walking?   (1)
2. What did they see hanging from a gate?   (2)
3. What happened to Decius while they were looking?   (2)
4. What did Publius do? Whom did he find?   (4)
5. What did one soldier ask (24)?   (2)
6. Why did the soldier not believe Publius' reply (25–26)?   (2)
7. Why was it hard to find the weapon?   (2)

CHAPTER 20

AGRICOLA IN BRITAIN

Agricola, who had been consul in 77 A.D., was sent out to Britain the next year as governor and commander. His first summer he conquered the Ordovices in North Wales and reduced the isle of Mona (Anglesey). In the next three years he advanced northwards, gradually conquering and pacifying the tribes in the north of England and the south of Scotland. It was not, of course, England and Scotland in those days. The country was Britannia, the northern part of it was called Caledonia and its people Caledonii Britanni, Caledonii for short.

He reached the Forth and the Clyde and built a chain of forts between them. In 82 he advanced towards Ireland but we do not know exactly where. Probably he crossed the Clyde and reconnoitred Argyll. The next year (83 A.D.) he advanced up the east side of the country. He was marching with his army in three divisions and one night the enemy attacked the camp of the ninth legion, the smallest. Agricola brought help in time to convert defeat into victory.

The next summer (84 A.D.) he advanced further and fought a great battle against the Scottish chief, Calgacus, at an unknown place called Mons Graupius. Although outnumbered, the Romans won. Agricola then sent his fleet to circumnavigate Britain.

The following year he was recalled by the Emperor Domitian and no Roman army ever penetrated so far north again.

20 A   **MARCUS IN SCOTLAND**

Six months passed before any more letters came from Marcus. The first three that he had written before he crossed to Britain never reached home. Now at last two arrived from Scotland.

MARCUS PATRI S.D.P.

tandem ad exercitum veni, undecimo die postquam Eboracum reliquimus. Agricola me benigne accepit et postridie ad nonam legionem misit. sum tribunus laticlavius in hac legione.

castra nostra sunt in magno campo qui est inter Bodotriam et montes. 5
in montibus habitant gentes feroces quae impetus in copias nostras saepe faciunt. aestate Agricola totum exercitum contra has gentes ducet. Agricola est dux magnus quem et milites et tribuni amant. omnes magnam spem gloriae praedaeque habemus.

dies (5) = day	*copiae (plur.) = forces*
legio (legionis) = legion	*aestas (aestatis) = summer*
campus = plain	*spes (5) = hope*
gens (gentis) = tribe	*praeda = plunder*

60

ceteri tribuni me benigne acceperunt. unus tamen, Quintus Lutetius, 10
me non amat, quod aliquid de Gallis dixi. Quintus enim est gentis
Gallicae, quamquam est civis Romanus. hoc tamen nesciebam.

paucis diebus postquam ad exercitum veni, iter in silvas venatum
fecimus. multi enim cervi et apri sunt in silvis. lupi quoque sunt
quorum ululatus nocte audimus. centum milites nobiscum venerunt. 15
hostes igitur nos vitaverunt. quinque cervos et unum aprum cepimus,
nec tamen lupos vidimus.

salutem multam matri et Iuliae et Tullo dices. vale.

aliquid = something	*aper = boar*
quamquam = although	*lupus = wolf*
nescio = I do not know	*ululatus(4) = howl*
venatum = hunting	*centum = a hundred*
cervus = deer	

20 B MARCUS' FIRST BATTLE

MARCUS PATRI S.D.P.

pugna magna fuit. hostes impetum in legionem nonam nocte fecerunt.
vulnus iterum accepi. sed rem totam tibi narrabo.

contra hostes iter faciebamus. Agricola exercitum in tres partes
diviserat. tertia nocte hostes castra nostra oppugnaverunt, fortasse 5
quod legio nostra est minima.

dormiebam. somniabam de Albatis. omnes 'Albati!' clamabant. subito
expergiscor. clamorem magnum et clangorem audio. statim surgo.
gladium rapio. subito hostis in tabernaculum meum ruit, Caledonius
magnus et hirsutus. me non statim videt. gladium in os eius inmitto. 10
ululat et ad terram cadit. iterum ferio. non movet.

e tabernaculo ruo. in omnibus partibus castrorum hostes cum
Romanis pugnant. subito barbarum video qui tabernaculum Quinti
Lutetii intrat. dormitne Quintus? intro et tergum barbari gladio
transfigo. Quintus nihil dicit sed una ad hostes currimus. duas horas 15
pugnamus. tandem prima luce Agricola cum ceteris copiis ad auxilium
venit. iam impetus in hostes et a fronte et a tergo facimus. illi tamen
fortiter resistunt. tandem fugiunt.

pugna = fight (noun)	*hirsutus = hairy*
res (5) = thing	*os (oris, N) = face*
minima = the smallest	*ferio = I strike*
somnio (1) = I dream	*tergum = back*
expergiscor = I wake up	*una = together*
tabernaculum = tent	*fortiter = bravely*

ubi lux venit, manum dextram sanguine perfusam vidi. gladius eam
ceciderat nec tamen est vulnus grave.   20

haec fuit prima pugna mea. vicimus. vivo. hoc tamen me vexat.
Quintus Lutetius, quod vitam eius servavi, me etiam magis odit. vale.

perfusam = covered   magis = more
ceciderat = had cut   odit = hates
vivo = I live

ROMAN CAMPS

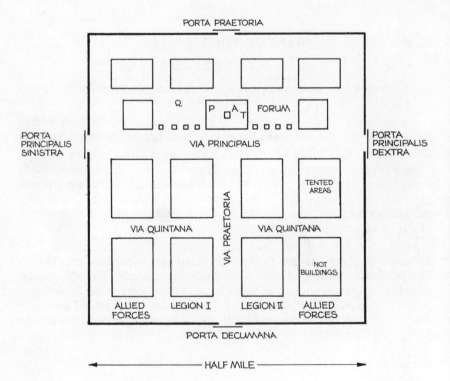

The diagram above is of a two legion camp. P marks the PRAETORIUM,
the general's tent and area. Near by was the AUGURALE (marked A),
an altar for taking the omens; also the TRIBUNAL (marked T), a platform
from which the general could address the troops assembled in the

FORUM. The other side of the praetorium was the QUAESTORIUM (marked Q), an area allotted to the quaestor, the officer in charge of supplies. The small squares represent tribunes' tents. The four gates were barriers rather than gates on hinges.

A group of eight men, called a CONTUBERNIUM, shared a tent. Eighty men in ten tents made up a century and the centurion commanding them had a larger tent at the end of the line.

The Roman army marched about twenty miles a day in five hours, always leaving time to fortify a camp for the night. The camp always had the same lay-out so that every man knew exactly where to go.

A tribune was sent ahead with a detachment of troops to choose a site. A good site would be on open ground, slightly sloping for good drainage, near water and pasture. With flags and spears they marked out the main points and roads. A ditch (FOSSA) was dug and the material used to form a rampart (AGGER) which was strengthened with turves. Each soldier carried two or three stakes and these were planted close together in the top of the rampart to form a fence about five feet high. If the enemy was near, half the soldiers stood guard while the rest built the ramparts.

VOCABULARY 20

hōra	= hour	tergum	= back
pugna	= fight	rēs (5)	= thing
vigilia	= watch	diēs (5,M)	= day
cōpiae (plur.)	= forces	merīdiēs (5,M)	= noon
campus	= plain	spēs (5)	= hope
aestās (aestātis, F)	= summer	medius	= middle
legiō (legiōnis, F)	= legion	nūntiō (1)	= I announce
gens (gentis, F)	= tribe	vīvō (3)	= I live
ōs (ōris, N)	= { face	nesciō (4)	= I not know
	mouth	fortiter	= bravely

Exercise 20 X   Questions about 20 B, lines 4–11.

1. Lines 4–6. In how many divisions was the army marching? What reason does Marcus suggest why the enemy attacked his legion's camp? (3)
2. Where was Marcus? What was he dreaming? What woke him? What did he do first? Who rushed in? What did Marcus do? What was the result? (12)

THE FIFTH DECLENSION

In this chapter come Fifth Declension nouns. They decline like RES (Grammar page 6). All Fifth Declension nouns are feminine except Dies (=day) and Meridies (=noon), which are masculine.

Exercise 20 C

1. avus meus ante meridiem numquam surgit.
2. nihil de his rebus scio.
3. magnam partem diei frustra consumpsimus.
4. quam spem habemus? hostes vicerunt.
5. iter decem dierum per montes fecimus.
6. I shall report the matter to your father.
7. We shall come to the camp* after noon.
8. What shall I do? Where are my hopes?
9. It is difficult to do big things quickly.

*Castra goes like the plural of Bellum.

NUMERALS

Learn the cardinals 30–3000, the ordinals 11th–20th and the numeral adverbs on page 1 of the Grammar. Learn the declension of Unus, Duo and Tres and the other information about numerals on page 11 of the Grammar.

Exercise 20 D

1. cum tribus amicis.
2. centum urbes.
3. id ter dixisti.
4. mille templa.
5. quadraginta milites.
6. est nona hora.
7. tria milia militum.
8. triginta custodes.
9. cum duabus sororibus.
10. quattuor milia hominum.
11. quinquaginta dies.
12. ducentas naves habet.
13. Gallos bis vicimus.
14. tertia vigilia veniam.
15. legio vicensima venit.

TIME

(a) *TIME WHEN:* The Ablative is the case used for the time *when* something happens.
Example: PRIMA HORA = AT THE FIRST HOUR.

(b) *TIME HOW LONG:* The Accusative is the case used for *how long* something happens.
Example: DECEM ANNOS = FOR TEN YEARS.

Note: *NO PREPOSITIONS* are used for 'on the fourth day', 'for three hours', etc.

The Romans divided the day (6.0 a.m. to 6.0 p.m.) into twelve hours, so dawn (prima lux) was at 6.0 a.m., the first hour (prima hora) from 6.0 to 7.0 and so on. The night they often divided not into hours but into four watches of three hours each, so the first watch (prima vigilia) was from 6.0 pm. to 9.0 p.m. and so on.

Exercise 20 E

1. tres horas Romani fortiter pugnaverunt.
2. tertia hora hostium copiae discesserunt.
3. hi gemini septem annos nati sunt.
4. media nocte e portu navigavimus.
5. diem noctemque tabellarius iter fecit.
6. secunda vigilia custodes periculum nuntiaverunt.
7. cur fles? brevi tempore reveniam.
8. illa aestate Agricola Ordovices vicit.

Exercise 20 F

1. They were fighting for five hours.
2. We departed at the fifth hour.
3. The Greeks and Trojans had fought for nine years.
4. In the tenth year the Greeks won.
5. Julia was ill for twelve days.
6. On the fourth day we came to a river.
7. We shall depart from the city at dawn.
8. In the third watch the enemy made an attack.
9. He has not slept for four nights.
10. I shall come back to the camp at noon.

OTHER EXERCISES

Exercise 20 G
1. Give acc. sing. of:— genu, res, sol, vulnus, sanguis.
2. Give gen. sing. of:— dies, exercitus, senex, aestas, Iuppiter.
3. Give abl. sing. of:— spes, lux, tempestas, impetus, vis.
4. Give abl. plur. of:— manus, dies, gens, copiae, castra.
5. Give acc. plur. of:— campus, os, genu, hora, iter.
6. Give gen. plur. of:— legio, gradus, dies, pugna, nuntius.

Exercise 20 H   Additional Practice.
1. For four days there was a big storm.
2. The enemy had attacked with great force.
3. It will be difficult to build so high a wall.
4. Now is the time for brave soldiers to fight.
5. We seized our arms and made an attack.
6. Both yesterday and today you fought bravely.
7. Neither the Romans nor the Britons will seek peace.
8. We shall make two attacks at dawn.

Exercise 20 I   Translate the words underlined. *Use Latin WORDS.*
Symbols are used here to save space.

1. You have one life.
2. He has 400 ships.
3. With two friends.
4. I've done it twice.
5. We were the first.
6. I see 20 tables.
7. It has three heads.
8. With fifty ships.
9. With three ships.
10. With 100 ships.
11. She is the third daughter.
12. He has 1000 soldiers.
13. There are 3000 enemy.
14. 200,000 citizens voted.
15. There are eleven cities.
16. He wrote 200 letters.
17. With 1000 soldiers.
18. We found 200 arrows.
19. It is the twelfth night.
20. I've said so three times.

Exercise 20 J   Practice at Pronouns.
1. illos flores non emam.
2. cenam tibi paravimus.
3. para cibum huic militi.
4. nobiscum non veniet.
5. quid cupit? eum nescio.
6. eorum ducem video.
7. rex eos condemnavit.
8. haec verba dixit.
9. quis vestrum veniet?
10. eius pater vivit.

Exercise 20 K CROSSWORD (All answers are in Latin)

CLUES ACROSS

1. Capitol hill of the capital city.
7. Slowly.
8. High and deep.
9. To.
11. They make beautiful garlands but first cut off the thorns.
13. Ghosts.
15. An entangling collection of holes joined together with rope.
18. English feminine horse makes Latin neuter sea.
19. Journey.
20. They contained multi-storey, miniaturized, postmortem accommodation.

CLUES DOWN

1. The hot spot at the Baths.
2. Horatius defended one over the Tiber.
3. Places where plays are acted.
4. Happy.
5. One.
6. In schools these rooms have pegs, not niches.
10. I crash.
12. Then a province around Carthage, now a continent.
14. I was a feminine horse backwards.
16. And.
17. You are the object.

CHAPTER 21

ROMAN MARRIAGES

Some time before the marriage a betrothal took place (SPONSALIA). The maiden was promised to the man by her father and they exchanged presents. The most usual present for the man to give the girl was a ring. This was worn on the third finger of the left hand because it was believed that a nerve ran directly from this finger to the heart.

On the eve of her wedding the bride dedicated to the Lares her toys and her bulla. It was considered lucky for her to sleep in the TUNICA RECTA, the old-fashioned, white tunic which she wore for her wedding. The next morning her mother helped her to dress. The tunic was fastened round her waist with a band of wool tied with a knot of Hercules which only the husband might untie. Her hair was divided into six locks with the point of a spear and then kept in position by ribbons. Over all she wore a flame-coloured veil (FLAMMEUM).

Carpets were spread at the entrance of the bride's house and it was hung with ribbons and flowers and wreaths of myrtle and laurel. Before dawn a sheep or pig was sacrificed and the omens taken, then the guests arrived in the atrium and waited for the bride and bridegroom. The marriage contract was signed and the hands of the bride and groom were joined and the bride pronounced the words: 'Ubi tu Gaius, ego Gaia'. All shouted 'Feliciter!' (Good Luck!) After this came the wedding feast which lasted all day. MUSTACEUS (wedding cake) was distributed.

Towards evening the bridegroom pretended to seize his bride and she to cling to her mother. This was the signal for the bride to be escorted to the bridegroom's house. Two boys held her hands and a third carried a torch in front of her. The wedding hymn (HYMENAEUS) was sung. Anyone might join the procession and all cried 'Talassio!' Nuts were thrown to the crowd.

When they reached the bridegroom's house, the bride wound wool round the doorposts and anointed the door with oil and fat. Then she was carried over the threshold by her attendants. She again pronounced the words 'Ubi tu Gaius, ego Gaia' and the husband offered his wife fire and water. She was then placed on the bridal couch which stood in the atrium and the guests went home. The next day the wife received presents from her husband and they gave a party (REPOTIA).

iam dies nuptialis venit. hodie Sextus Flaviam in matrimonium ducit.
Tullus et Iulia cum parentibus invitati sunt. ante primam lucem surgunt
et iter breve faciunt. ubi adveniunt, stant et domum spectant. ianua
vittis et floribus decorata est, postes myrto lauroque ornati sunt.

omnes in atrium ducuntur. omnes a Calpurnia, matre Flaviae, et a 5
Flavio patre accipiuntur. mox Flavia intrat, mox Sextus. tabulae
nuptiales signantur. dextrae manus Flaviae Sextique iunguntur.

'quid est nomen tuum?' rogat Sextus.

'ubi tu Gaius, ego Gaia,' respondet Flavia.
omnes 'feliciter!' clamant.   10

iam cena nuptialis parata est. Tullus et Iulia cum parentibus sedent.
Tullus non modo multum cibi consumit sed etiam vinum bibit. multum
cibi ab omnibus consumitur; multum vini bibitur. omnes rident, omnes
sunt laeti. tandem mustaceus distribuitur. subito Sextus Flaviam rapit
et ad ianuam portat. omnes surgunt atque in viam festinant. Sextus et 15
Flavia per vias deducuntur. nuces coniciuntur. Hymenaeus cantatur 'io
Hymen! Hymenaee io!' omnes cantant, omnes rident, omnes 'Talassio!'
clamant.

ubi adveniunt, Sextus primus intrat. inde Flavia super limen portatur
atque a Sexto igni et aqua accipitur. iterum Sextus rogat 'quid est 20
nomen tuum?' iterum Flavia respondet 'ubi tu Gaius, ego Gaia.' omnes
atrium intrant.

subito Aemilia Lucio 'ubi est Tullus?' inquit. Lucius circumspectat.
Iuliam conspicit nec tamen Tullum.

'Iulia,' rogat 'ubi est Tullus?'   25

Iulia 'nescio,' respondet. 'in via constitit quod felem claudam quam
canes vexabant vidit.'

'o stultum puerum!' clamat Lucius. 'cur nobiscum non mansit?'

nuptialis = wedding (adj.)	deduco = I escort
advenio = I arrive	nuces = nuts
vitta = ribbon	super limen = over the threshold
a = by	ignis = fire
tabulae nuptiales = marriage	conspicio = I catch sight of, see
contract	consisto (perf. constiti) = I stop, halt
iungo = I join	feles (felis, F) = cat
modo = only	claudus = lame
atque = and	

ubi est Tullus? Lucius in viam contendit et circumspectat. a Laevino comitatus est. Tullum non conspiciunt; multi tamen homines sunt in via. per viam celeriter ambulant et puerum quaerunt. Lucius anxius est quod viae Romanae pueris periculosae sunt. in gradibus templi puella sedebat et flores vendebat. Lucius consistit et rogat: 5

'vidistine puerum capillo nigro, octo annos natum, et felem claudam?'

'ita vero,' respondet puella. 'puer qui felem portabat in illam viam processit.'

Lucius pecuniam puellae dat atque in viam quam puella 10 demonstravit festinat. Tullum non conspicit. tres senes sub arbore stabant.

'vidistisne puerum capillo nigro, octo annos natum, et felem claudam?'

unus e senibus 'ego' inquit 'puerum capillo nigro vidi. erat cum 15 mercatore Aegyptio, nomine Narbarse. illam tabernam intraverunt. felem non vidi.'

'eheu!' clamat Laevinus. 'Narbarses est venalicius. Tullum rapiet atque in servitutem vendet.'

contendo = I hurry, march	procedo (perf. processi) = I
vendo = I sell	proceed, go on
capillus = hair	arbor = tree
	venalicius = slave-dealer

Exercise 21 X Questions about 21 B.

1. Who accompanied Lucius on his search? (1)
2. Who was sitting on the steps of the temple? What was she doing? (2)
3. What did Lucius ask her? Answer fully. (4)
4. What did she reply? (2)
5. How did he thank her? (2)
6. Whom did he see standing under a tree? (2)
7. What information did he receive from them? (5)
8. Why did this information horrify Laevinus? (2)

THE PASSIVE VOICE

When the verb is active, the subject is doing something (e.g. The cat mews); when the verb is passive, the subject is having something done to it (e.g. The cat is stroked).

A passive verb has no object.

In this chapter you meet the Present and Perfect passive of all conjugations: Grammar pages 20 & 22.

The first Principal Part is used to form the Present Passive and the last one to form the Perfect Passive.

Exercise 21 C

1. amatur.
2. moniti estis.
3. a te docemur.
4. milites celati sunt.
5. vinum hic venditur.
6. in periculum ducimur.
7. murus aedificatus est.
8. non audiris.
9. He has been warned.
10. They are loved.
11. You have been wounded.
12. They are being taught.
13. A port was fortified.
14. We are not being heard.
15. We have been frightened.
16. It is being finished.

THE PERFECT PASSIVE OF IRREGULAR VERBS

It does not matter what conjugation a verb is, *the last principal part is used:*

E.g. missum gives missus sum.

Exercise 21 D

1. missus es.
2. rogati sumus (*not irreg.*)
3. iuncti sunt.
4. visus sum.
5. occisus est.
6. accepti sunt.
7. victi estis.
8. relicti sumus.
9. He has been seen.
10. He has been praised (*not irreg.*)
11. He has been abandoned.
12. He has been captured.
13. The soldiers have been led.
14. You have been taught.
15. We have been sent.
16. The food has been touched.

A = BY

With people and animals the preposition 'A' ('AB' if it sounds better) is used for 'BY' followed by the Ablative. With things the Ablative only is used.

E.g. Gladio necatus est = He was killed by a sword.

A me necatus est = He was killed by me.

Exercise 21 E Translate the words underlined.

1. Defended by a ditch.
2. Killed by the consul.
3. Hidden by a cloud.
4. Mauled by lions
5. Helped by his sisters.
6. Wounded by an arrow.
7. We beat them by sea.
8. Praised by the general.

Exercise 21 F

1. nonne hic liber a te scriptus est?
2. mercator a duobus militibus custoditur.
3. frater meus et capite et manu et genu vulneratus est.
4. ab nobis omnibus amaris, o rex magne.
5. Galli impetu nostro territi sunt.
6. omnes ab imperatore laudati estis.
7. civis Romanus sum. cur leonibus conicior?
8. et a Gallis et a Britannis timemur.
9. ubi tres horas contenderunt, constiterunt.
10. praemia omnibus servis dantur.

Exercise 21 G *(No object accusatives with passives).*

1. Our forces are led by the two consuls.
2. Shouts were heard by all the boys.
3. The city is being fortified with a high wall.
4. We are taught by a good master.
5. Fires are sighted every-day on the mountain.
6. We were received kindly by the queen.
7. There is no hope. You have been seen by the enemy.
8. I have never been frightened by storms.
9. The little girl sells flowers in the street.
10. A high wall has been built round the city*.

* *acc. after circum, NOT an object accusative.*

VOCABULARY 21

rēgīna	=queen	iungō (3)	=I join
praemium	=reward	contendō (3) =	{ I hurry,
arbor (arboris, F)	=tree		I march
ignis (ignis, M)	=fire	cōnsistō (3)	=I halt
terreō (2)	=I frighten	prōcēdō (3)	=I proceed
conspiciō (3½)	=I see	vēndō (3)	=I sell
adveniō (4)	=I arrive	ā, ab (+abl)	=by
custōdiō (4)	=I guard	atque	=and
		modo	=only

OTHER EXERCISES:

Exercise 21 H   Questions about 21 A

1. Give an English word derived from: primam (2), ducuntur (5), dextrae (7).
2. Give nom. sing. of:— lucem (2), floribus (4).
3. Give gen. sing. of:— iter breve (3), dextrae manus (7).
4. In what case is:— dies (1), parentibus (2), nomen (8)?
5. Give 1st. sing. pres. act. of:— venit (1), ducuntur (5).
6. Give pres. infinitive of:— faciunt (3), stant (3).
7. Put into the future:— ducit (1), spectant (3), (For example 'stat' becomes 'stabit' and 'rego' becomes 'regam').
8. Put into the perfect:— intrat (6), faciunt (3).

CODES

Codes were used in ancient times to keep messages secret. Julius Caesar used to substitute for each letter the one that stood three places lower in the alphabet. Other more complicated codes were used but substitution of letters (not always having the same position relative to the real letter) was the commonest.

Exercise 21 I   Can you decipher this letter?

UFEKT GMKNS T.A.D.
DPOKREF PTN OPCFNF ER DKNPS ER FMPF ZECCFP. NP LPAEF RSONP ER TECZF DMSDP OFNFMFONFL PITDPONFGS.

ZFCP.

CHAPTER 22

DASH TO OSTIA

sine mora Lucius et Laevinus in tabernam contenderunt. multi homines
ibi bibebant.

'vidistisne puerum et mercatorem Aegyptium?' clamavit Laevinus.

'ubi est Narbarses?' clamavit Lucius. multa responsa data sunt.

'nullum puerum vidi.'   5

'qui estis?'

'vinum puero ab Narbarse dabatur.'

'Narbarsem nescio.'

'cur puerum quaeris?'

'puer dormiebat. Aegyptius eum e taberna portavit.'   10

'Narbarses discessit.'

caupo nihil dixit.

'o me miserum!' clamavit Lucius. 'Narbarses vinum medicamento
mixtum Tullo dedit.'

Laevinus 'cras prima luce,' inquit 'ingens numerus navium e portu   15
Ostia ad Aegyptum navigabit. festinare debemus.' e taberna ruerunt.

'voca vigiles!' clamavit Lucius. 'Bassus, amicus tuus, est praefectus
vigilum. ego omnes servos meos excitabo et ad portum contendam.'

Lucius, ubi ad portum Ostiam venit, naves quae ad navigandum
parabantur celeriter invenit. ad navem ingentem contendit et nautae   20
clamavit: 'ubi est Narbarses? estne in nave tua? negotium cum eo
habeo.'

'Narbarses abest sed mox reveniet.'

Lucius et servi non procul ab nave impatientes exspectaverunt. mox
homo appropinquavit. corpus portabat.   25

'quem in navem portas?' rogavit Lucius. 'estne Tullus, filius meus?'

mercator audax risit. 'non est filius tuus,' respondit. 'est filius nautae.
fessus est. dormit. si cupis, inspice eum.'

puerum ostendit. non erat Tullus. capillum nigrum habebat et Tullo
similis erat nec tamen erat Tullus.   30

sine = without	ad navigandum = for sailing
mora = delay	negotium = business
caupo = innkeeper	absum = am absent
ingens = huge	audax = bold
vigiles (plural) = the watch	ostendo = I show
praefectus = commander	capillus = hair
excito = I wake	

puer non erat Tullus. Lucius stetit attonitus. nihil dixit. Aegyptius risit et puerum in navem portavit. subito Laevinus cum Publio Basso et viginti vigilibus advenit. Lucius rem celeriter explicavit.

Laevinus 'fortasse' inquit 'hic est alius puer qui ab Narbarse captus est. fortasse Tullus in navem iam portatus est.' 5

Bassus 'ita vero' inquit. 'vigiles navem inspicere iubebo.' signum dedit. sine mora vigiles navem ascenderunt, quamquam Narbarses nautas resistere iussit.

subito servus ad Lucium cucurrit.

'o domine, te inveni. duas horas te quaero. ab Aemilia missus sum. 10 Tullus est salvus. ad nuptias revenit paullo postquam discessisti.'

interea Bassus et vigiles e nave descendebant. quinque pueri a vigilibus portabantur, quorum quattuor dormiebant. unus tamen clamabat 'servate me! servate me! in servitutem me vendent.'

ei Bassus 'nemo' inquit 'te vendet, mi amice. es puer felix.' inde 15 vigilibus 'comprehendite Narbarsem. tenete hanc navem in portu.'

Lucius domum festinavit Tullumque magno gaudio vidit. Aemilia eum anxia exspectabat.

'ecce Tullus,' inquit. 'numquam in periculo fuit. ad nuptias mox revenit.' 20

Lucius uxori rem totam narravit. Aemilia, ubi de venalicio et pueris audivit, attonita erat; Tullus tamen iram patris timuit.

'ego' inquit 'Aegyptium numquam vidi. ego tabernam numquam intravi. non diu aberam. felem claudam quae a canibus vexabatur servabam. num me culpas?' 25

pater risit. 'te non culpo.' inquit. 'non modo feles a te hodie servata est sed etiam quinque pueri qui in servitutem rapiebantur.'

explico = I explain	felix = lucky
iubeo = I order	comprehendo = I arrest
quamquam = although	gaudium = joy
salvus = safe	uxor = wife
paullo = a little	culpo = I blame

TRADE AND TRAVEL

Rome with a population of over a million was the biggest market in the ancient world. Some things, such as metal ware, jewellery and luxury goods were manufactured there and exported. Far more were imported:— corn, glassware and papyrus from Egypt, perfumes from Arabia, silk from China, amber from Germany, metals from Spain, purple dye from Syria, wild beasts from Africa. There was a big slave-market in Rome near the Forum but, of course, boys who had been kidnapped would be taken and sold far away.

RAEDA

PLAUSTRUM

Ostia was the port of Rome and an industrial city too. From Ostia a boat could travel to Carthage in three days or to Alexandria in ten, much depending on the weather.

It was easier to send goods by water than by land so rivers and canals were used as well as the sea. By land goods went by waggon. The army used the 'carrus', which was faster than most waggons. For really heavy goods, such as barrels of wine or stone for building, the low-slung 'serracum' was used. The most commonly seen waggon was the 'plaustrum' which had two solid, wooden wheels; it was used on farms and for bringing farm produce into the cities.

Many travellers liked to go by sea but there were disadvantages: (1) boats were small and uncomfortable, especially in rough weather; (2) because they had no compass, captains often followed the coast, which made the journey longer; (3) there were usually no boats sailing in winter; (4) boats did not leave and arrive at regular times as they do today. If you were not rich enough to charter a boat, you had to wait until one was going your way, then make an arrangement with the captain.

Many preferred to go by land and if going from Rome to Athens, rather than go by sea from Ostia, would go by road to Brundisium, then make the short sea crossing to Dyracchium, then continue by land. Roman roads were better than any others until recent times. The roadway (fifteen feet wide and three feet deep) was built up above the level of the country through which it passed and was slightly cambered so that the rain drained off. Each side there was a ditch. The road went as straight as possible: hills were cut or tunnelled, bridges or causeways were used at rivers, viaducts or mattresses of logs carried it over marshy ground. Trees were cut back to prevent ambushes. There were milestones and at intervals fountains for men and water-troughs for animals.

There were inns (cauponae) but they were dirty and dangerous. Those who could stayed with friends (HOSPITES). A man had friends in as many towns as possible. When he was in a foreign town, he stayed with one of them; when one of his friends was in his town, he stayed with him. Thus the word 'hospes' can mean 'host' or 'guest'. These valuable 'guest-friendships' were passed down from father to son.

A traveller wore a heavy woollen cloak (paenula), carried his belongings in a leather bag and had a purse (marsupium) attached to his belt. He also carried a weapon or at least a stout stick. On lonely stretches men travelled in groups for fear of bandits. Officials had military escorts.

A litter (lectica), carried by eight sturdy slaves, was a comfortable method of travelling but was expensive and slow. A man walking might cover twenty-five miles a day, in a light vehicle forty to fifty. There were various types of vehicle. Two commonly in use were:— the 'raeda', a large, slow, covered four-wheeler for transporting a family and their baggage; the 'cisium', a light two-wheeler for a man with little baggage.

Many people travelled on horse or mule. However one went, there was dust in summer and mud in winter; there was jolting and boredom. 'They arrived travel-stained and weary' was a more meaningful phrase in those days.

CISIUM

POLICE AND FIREMEN IN ROMAN TIMES

In the provinces each Governor was responsible for law and order and used soldiers to enforce them. In the western provinces and in Italy trade-guilds undertook the task of fire-fighting but in the eastern provinces such guilds did not exist. When Pliny, the governor of Bithynia, suggested starting a fire-brigade, the Emperor Trajan said 'No. All organized groups become political. Provide the equipment and let property owners and the populace deal with fires.'

In Rome itself there were no police in Republican times and there were often riots. Augustus, the first Emperor, enrolled 7000 vigiles (watchmen). These were firemen, though they had a few police duties. Their commander (praefectus vigilum) was a knight (eques) appointed by the Emperor. They were divided into seven cohorts and stationed in the various districts of Rome. Ostia had no vigiles until the Emperor Hadrian enrolled some.

Augustus also enrolled three 'cohortes urbanae' (urban cohorts), commanded by a 'praefectus urbi' (city prefect). These were soldiers whose duty was to keep order in Rome and they were Rome's nearest equivalent to police.

There were no detectives. The Emperor and his magistrates relied on informers. Lawyers investigated matters for their clients.

VOCABULARY 22

mora	= delay	culpō (1)	= I blame
gaudium	= joy	iubeō (2)	= I order
uxor (uxōris)	= wife	instruō (3)	= I draw up
ingēns	= huge	ostendō (3)	= I show
sapiēns	= wise	comprehendō (3)	= I arrest
fēlīx	= fortunate	absum (sum)	= I am absent
audāx	= bold	sine (+ abl.)	= without
vēlōx	= swift	facile	= easily
ferōx	= fierce	quamquam	= although
appellō (1)	= I name		

IMPERFECT PASSIVE

In this chapter you meet the Imperfect Passive (Grammar page 22). This is an easily recognized tense and all conjugations have the same endings.

CHANGE OF ENDING IN THE PASSIVE

Where a passive tense consists of two words, such as Amatus sum, the first word, amatus, declines like Bonus and is feminine or neuter if the subject is feminine or neuter.
Examples:

puer laudatus est	pueri laudati sunt
puella laudata est	puellae laudatae sunt
vinum laudatum est	vina laudata sunt

Exercise 22 C

1. captus est.
2. capta est.
3. captum est.
4. verba scripta sunt.
5. non culpatus sum.
6. urbes munitae sunt.
7. tractum est.
8. visi estis.
9. castra capta sunt.
10. flores empti sunt.

11. The boy has been saved.
12. The girl has been saved.
13. The town has been saved.
14. Ships have been seen.
15. Signals have been seen.
16. Enemy have been seen.
17. A signal has been given.
18. She has been received.
19. He has been ordered.
20. It has been decided.

ADJECTIVES CONTINUED

In this chapter you learn Ingens and Felix (Grammar page 9) and other adjectives like them.

Exercise 22 D

Make ingens agree with:— portam, campum, caput, monte, navium.
Make felix agree with:—   ducis, sorore, regem, fratribus, reginarum.

Exercise 22 F

1. eorum urbs ab duce audaci oppugnabatur.
2. hi equi sunt veloces et acres.
3. num haec epistola ab eo scripta est?
4. copiae ingentes in campo ab Agricola instructae sunt.
5. eius manus a custodibus tenebantur.
6. ducem felicem omnes milites amant.
7. illud sine mora constitutum est.
8. a leone feroci in eam silvam tracta est.
9. a Polymathe, magistro sapienti, docebar.
10. et te et fratrem tuum comprehendere iussi sumus.

Exercise 22 F

1. The town has been captured by a bold attack.
2. You were being praised by all the citizens.
3. We are being led into battle by a lucky leader.
4. All the girls were delighted by the song.
5. You are ruled by a wise queen.
6. The city was being easily defended by a few soldiers.
7. Huge rocks were falling on to our heads.
8. The letters have been carried by a swift messenger.
9. Although I was absent, the boys were working.
10. The enemy camp (= camp of the enemy) has been captured by your plan.

OTHER EXERCISES

Exercise 22 G   Questions about 22 A

1. Give nom. sing. of: prima luce (15), omnes servos (18).
2. Give acc. plur. of: vinum (7), navium (15).
3. Give pres. infin of: data sunt (4), invenit (20).
4. 1st. sing. pres. act.: est (4), discessit (11).
5. Put into imperf.: contenderunt (1), venit (19).
6. What case is: mora (1), portu (15)?
7. Give a word derived from: vidistis (3), dixit (12), vigiles (17).
8. To whom or what do the pronouns ferer:- eum (10), me (13), eo (21)?

WHO KILLED CANIDIA?

Exercise 22 H

Make out the following. Look up words you don't know in the vocabulary.

in urbe Roma incendia erant crebra. vigiles numquam erant otiosi.

olim insula magna prope Amphitheatrum Flavium nocte incensa est. quod incendium erat magnum, Bassus ipse, praefectus vigilum, aderat. centum vigiles flammas exstinguere temptabant. viae erant hominum plenae. feminae ululabant, viri bona sua in plaustra ponebant. alii 5 fugiebant, alii in cenacula revenire temptabant liberos uxoresque petitum.

tandem flammae exstinctae sunt. vigiles intraverunt. mox corpora ex insula portabantur. duodecim perierant, quinque viri, tres feminae, quattuor liberi. 10

unus e vigilibus ad Bassum contendit et 'femina' inquit 'inventa est cuius pectus pugione transfixum est.' 'quis est?' rogat Bassus.

VIG	ego in insula proxima habito. multas res de ea scio. Canidia appellatur. maritus eius miles fuit sed occisus est. sola habitat sed Philerastus, mercator Graecus qui tabernam unguentariam 15 habet, eam saepe visitat. ipsa in caupona quae est in insula laborat. caupo Gullus appellatur. Canidia multam pecuniam Abileni, mercatori Syrio qui est dominus insulae debet.
BASS	bene fecisti. tege corpus. nihil de hoc dicemus. omnes qui in illa insula habitant singulatim interrogare cupio, primum eos 20 qui Canidiam noverant. *haw known.*
VIG	cenaculum meum proximum est. parvum est sed mundum. facile erit tibi homines singulatim in eo interrogare.
BASS	multas gratias.

(ad cenaculum contendunt. mercator Graecus inducitur.) 25

PHIL	o domine, quid faciam? tota taberna mea incensa est. omnia unguenta mea perierunt.
BASS	tace! paucas res te rogare cupio. quid te nocte proxima excitavit? quando incendium sensisti?'
PHIL	media nocte fumum sensi. in viam cucurri. flammas vidi. 30 insulam iterum intravi scalasque ascendere temptavi. flammae tamen me reppulerunt.
BASS	cur scalas ascendere temptavisti?
PHIL	Canidiam, amicam meam, servare cupivi. ubi est Canidia? num incendio periit? 35
BASS	unum corpus pugione transfixum est. quid de hoc scis?
PHIL	nihil scio. ubi est Canidia?
BASS	corpora ex insula portata sunt. mox ea inspicere licebit.

(Philerastus educitur. Gullus et uxor inducuntur.)

81

BASS	quid vos excitavit? quando incendium sensistis? 40
GULL	Gaia me excitavit. 'surge!' clamabat. 'incendium est. porta omnes res in viam!'
BASS	quid te excitavit et quando?
GAIA	crepitus flammarum me media nocte excitavit.
BASS	duodecim corpora a vigilibus inventa sunt. unum tamen pugione transfixum est. quid de hoc scis?
GAIA	fortasse a furibus necata est. multi fures insulas nocte intrant.
GULL	nihil scio. dormiebam.
BASS	satis. Abilenem, dominum insulae, interrogabo. (caupo et uxor educuntur. Abilenis inducitur.)
BASS	quid te nocte excitavit et quando?
ABIL	clamoribus excitatus sum post mediam noctem. in viam rui et multas flammas vidi. servos excitavi et eos vigiles petitum misi.
BASS	unum corpus pugione transfixum est. quid de hoc scis?
ABIL	quis est? num Blaesus? num Canidia? num Zoilus? hi omnes pecuniam mihi debent.
BASS	mox scies. mox omnes omnia sciemus. (exit Abilenis)
VIG	quattuor testes qui Canidiam noverant iam interrogavisti. sexaginta octo manent.
BASS	non necesse erit omnes interrogare. aliquis in suspicionem mihi iam venit.

Line numbers in right margin: 45, 50, 55, 60

WHOM DOES BASSUS SUSPECT AND WHY?

Exercise 22 I Questions about 22 H, lines 40–49.

1. Who did Gullus say woke him (41)? What was she shouting? (3)
2. Which of Bassus' questions (40) does Gullus not answer? (2)
3. What did Bassus ask Gaia (43)? What did she reply? (4)
4. How many bodies had been found by the watchmen? (1)
5. What did Gaia suggest had happened to the one that had been stabbed. (2)
6. What did Gullus say he knew? What reason did he give? (2)
7. Whom did Bassus question next? (1)

CHAPTER 23

23 A

AMBUSHED

MARCUS PATRI S.D.P.

si vales, bene est. ego valeo. in Caledonia hiemes sunt longissimae et frigidissimae. ubique silvae, montes, nubes. sol est rarior quam cycnus niger. hostes non saepe conspicimus, quamquam eos quaerimus. in unam tamen expeditionem missi sumus in qua in maximum periculum 5 adductus sum. sed rem totam tibi narrabo.

per silvas equitabamus. subito hostes impetum acerrimum in agmen fecerunt. alii sagittas in equos mittunt, alii de arboribus in equites desiliunt. unus in tergum meum desilit. ad terram cadimus. pugnamus. gladium meum stringere tempto sed frustra. Caledonius iugulum 10 meum manibus premit. manus eius duriores sunt quam ferrum. oculos claudo. dormio. subito manus relaxantur. oculos aperio. rem miram video. Caledonius nullum caput habet. Quintus adest. gladium sanguinolentum tenet. sanguine calido perfusus sum. gratias maximas Quinto ago atque equum celeriter peto. hostes tandem repellimus; 15 undecim tamen ex equitibus nostris sunt occisi.

quam miri sunt homines! Quintus, quod vitam meam servavit, me non iam odit. ex inimico amicus factus est. die cum eo equito, nocte cum eo bibo. nunc carior est mihi quam ceteri tribuni.

salutem multam matri et Iuliae et Tullo dices. 'feliciter' Sexto et 20 Flaviae dices. vale.

bene = well	iugulum = throat
hiems (hiemis) = winter	premo = I press
ubique = everywhere	durus = hard
quam = than	ferrum = iron
cycnus = swan	mirus = amazing
adduco = I bring	adsum = am present
agmen = column	perfusus = drenched
alii . . alii . . = some . . others . .	gratias ago = I give thanks, thank
eques (equitis) = rider, horseman	odit = hates
desilio = I jump down	inimicus = enemy
stringo = I draw	carus = dear

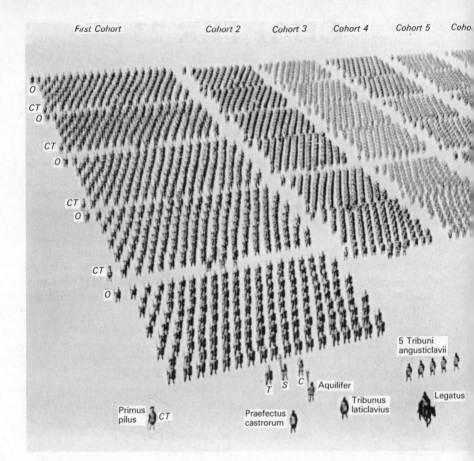

5 Tribuni angusticlavii

Aquilifer

T   S   C

Tribunus laticlavius

Legatus

Primus pilus   CT

Praefectus castrorum

THE ROMAN ARMY

The Roman army at the time of the Emperor Domitian consisted of 28 legions. Each legion had about 5500 men and was made up as follows:—

8 men	= 1 contubernium	8 men
80 men	= 1 century	80 men
2 centuries	= 1 maniple	160 men
3 maniples	= 1 cohort	c 500 men
10 cohorts	= 1 legion	c 5500 men

The first cohort consisted of five maniples (800 men). There was also a squadron of 120 horsemen who acted as scouts and dispatch-riders.

The commander of the legion (LEGATUS) was a senator, usually a man in his thirties, appointed by the Emperor. He was sometimes also governor of a province.

During the Republic the commander of an army could be an 'imperator' (general, commander-in-chief) but Augustus, the first

84

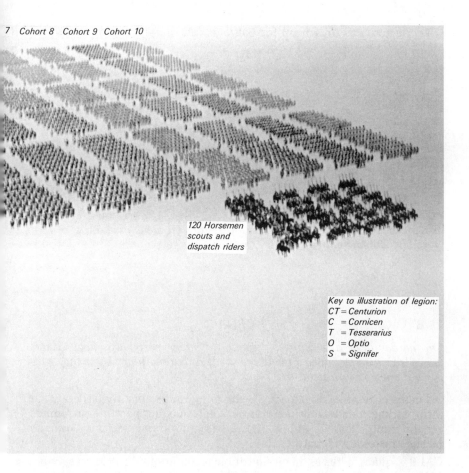

120 Horsemen
scouts and
dispatch riders

Key to illustration of legion:
CT = Centurion
C = Cornicen
T = Tesserarius
O = Optio
S = Signifer

Emperor, took the title for himself to show that he commanded the whole Roman army. His successors did the same and the word 'imperator' changed its meaning, giving us the word 'emperor'.

The backbone of the legion were the centurions, professional soldiers promoted from the ranks. The centurions of the first cohort were senior and the senior of these was the PRIMUS PILUS, a man of over fifty who served for one year at a very large salary. When a primus pilus retired, he might be promoted to PRAEFECTUS CASTRORUM (camp prefect), who organized the equipment and transport of the legion.

Junior to the centurions were:— OPTIO (sergeant), SIGNIFER (standard-bearer), AQUILIFER (standard-bearer of the legion), TESSERARIUS (password man), CORNICEN (trumpeter).

The tribunes (TRIBUNI) were young officers learning the profession of arms. How much responsibility they were given depended on the legatus.

The legion was drawn up for battle as follows:

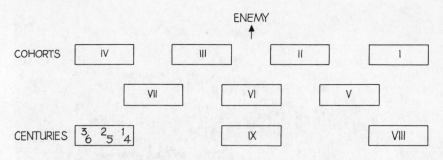

The auxiliary units, allied forces (AUXILIA) were raised in the provinces from non-citizens. Some of them were heavy infantry, others were specialists such as cavalry, archers, slingers.

23 B   **CENA**

On the day after a wedding a 'repotia' (drinking party) was held. Sextus cancelled theirs as Flavia's grandmother died that morning. Later they gave a big dinner party instead.

Lucius et Aemilia ad cenam a Sexto cum multis aliis invitati erant. in atrio multae mensae positae erant et cena maxima parata erat. omnes recubuerunt. Flavia et Sextus laetissimi erant. Lucius quoque laetissimus esse videbatur.

CALP	quam laetus es, Luci! sine dubio laetus es quod Tullus est salvus.	5
LUC	non modo Tullus sed etiam Marcus salvus est. epistolam ab eo hodie accepi. 'feliciter' Flaviae et Sexto dixit. vita eius a tribuno Gallico qui antea inimicus fuerat servata est.	
FLAV	cur inimicus Marci vitam servavit?	
CALP	Galli sunt mobiliores quam aqua.	10
ALEX	mobiliores quam puellae.	
LUC	sed fortissimi sunt.	
SEXT	ita vero. milites optimi sunt sed Britanni sunt meliores.	
LAEV	Britanni sunt feroces et duri sed disciplinam non habent.	
AUL	Galli sunt meliores. Galli Romanos ad Alliam vicerunt.	15
SEXT	maiores copias quam Romani habebant.	
LAEV	plurimos abhinc annos ad Alliam pugnatum est.	
LUC	Iulius Caesar Gallos minoribus copiis vicit.	
APP	Romani sunt optimi omnium militum.	
LAEV	sine dubio.	20

recumbo = I lie down	*mobilis = fickle*
dubius = doubt(ful)	*ad = at*
antea = before	*abhinc = ago*

LUC	nemo id dubitat.
FLAV	qui sunt milites pessimi?
AUL	Graeci.
APP	Graeci? insanus es. Athenienses minimis copiis maximum exercitum Persarum vicerunt. Alexander Magnus minimis 25 copiis innumerabiles exercitus superavit. Lacedaemonii omnium militum fortissimi fuerunt.
AUL	fuerunt. hodie Graeci fortiter non pugnant. quid tu dicis, Alexander?
ALEX	hodie non necesse est Graecis pugnare. Romani nos defen- 30 dunt. Romani sunt custodes nostri qui nos defendunt. Graeci sunt sapientiores quam Romani. non pugnant nisi necesse est.
AUL	quod dicis absurdum est. Romani sunt domini Graecorum. Romani Graecos vicerunt.
ALEX	non Graeci sed Macedones a Romanis victi sunt. Graeci 35 Romanos in Graeciam libenter acceperunt.
APP	Aegyptii sunt peiores quam Graeci.
AEM	gens venaliciorum.
LAEV	sub Pharaonibus Aegyptii fuerunt potentissimi.
LUC	olim Aegyptii erant potentes, inde Persae, inde Graeci, nunc 40 Romani. qui post ducentos annos erunt potentes? Romani?
MULT	Romani.
LUC	qui post duo milia annorum? Germani? Britanni?

sic multas horas sermo hilaris habebatur.

> *supero = I defeat*   *potens = powerful*
> *Lacedaemonius = Spartan*   *sic = so*
> *nisi = unless*   *sermo = conversation*
> *libenter = gladly*   *hilaris = cheerful*

Exercise 23 X Questions about 23 B, lines 21–34.

1. What does Flavia ask (22) and what does Aulus reply?   (3)
2. Appius disagrees (24–27). What three examples of brave Greeks does he give? What does he say about each?   (8)
3. What reason does Alexander give (30–32) why the Greeks don't fight in his day? Do you think it is a good reason? Say why.   (4)

PLUPERFECT PASSIVE

In this chapter you meet the Pluperfect Passive (Grammar page 23). It is formed from the Supine, e.g. missum gives missus eram.

Exercise 23 C *(Not all pluperfects)*

1. iussus eram.
2. constitimus.
3. domum vendet.
4. ignes facti erant.
5. consul aberat.
6. manus iunctae sunt.
7. mox adveniemus.
8. non instructi eramus.
9. lente processerint.
10. apertum erat.
11. He had been defeated.
12. The woman had been seen.
13. A reward has been given.
14. She had been blamed.
15. Arms had been prepared.
16. They are being arrested.
17. We are present.
18. They were marching.
19. Spears were being thrown.
20. It had been announced.

COMPARISON OF ADJECTIVES (MELIOR)

These can be found on page 10 of the Grammar. Type D (irregular) do not come in exercises until Chapter 24. Comparatives decline like Melior (Grammar page 9) and Superlatives decline like Bonus.
Two things being compared must be in the same case, e.g.
(1) Gaius est stultior quam tu. 'Gaius' is in the nom., therefore 'tu' is in the nom.
(2) Breviorem viam quam illam inveni. 'viam' is in the acc., therefore 'illam' is in the acc.

Exercise 23 D

Give the comparative and superlative of:—
altus, turpis, felix, sapiens, miser, difficilis, ferox, pulcher, fortis, saevus.

Exercise 23 E Translate the words underlined or the whole, as directed.

1. In a <u>deeper</u> ditch.
2. In a <u>very deep</u> ditch.
3. It is an <u>easier</u> task.
4. It is a <u>very easy</u> task.
5. By a <u>wiser</u> woman.
6. By a <u>very wise</u> queen.
7. She is <u>more beautiful.</u>
8. I see a <u>very ill</u> girl.
9. They are <u>heavier</u> burdens.
10. It is <u>very heavy.</u>

Exercise 23 F

1. hi equi sunt velociores quam tui.
2. turpe est fugere. turpius est dona ab hostibus accipere.
3. difficillimum erat et castra munire et cum hostibus pugnare.
4. milites audacissimi occisi erant.
5. canem ferociorem quam illum numquam vidi.
6. eorum equites a Lacedaemoniis victi erant.
7. ab aliis culparis, ab aliis laudaris.
8. sine dubio in Urbe cras adero.
9. in nave velociore quam vestra navigavimus.
10. quamquam superati eramus, non capti eramus.

Exercise 23 G

1. The old man is quicker than the young man.
2. We are very fortunate. We have very brave soldiers.
3. I have never seen a more beautiful girl than Melissa.
4. All our tasks are very easy.
5. Your bed is shorter than mine.
6. We are led by a very wise general.
7. The most beautiful slaves had been sold quickly.
8. We marched to the harbour by a longer road.
9. Your head is harder than the tree.
10. We had been ordered to advance through the mountains in winter.

VOCABULARY 23

grātiae	= thanks	cārus	= dear
grātiās agō	= I thank	dūrus	= hard
inimīcus	= enemy	mīrus	= amazing
Lacedaemonius	= Spartan	dubius	= doubtful
ferrum	= iron	quam	= than
eques (equitis, M)	= horseman	nisi	= unless
hiems (hiemis, F)	= winter	libenter	= gladly
superō (1)	= I defeat	sīc	= so, thus
adsum (sum)	= I am present	anteā	= before
aliī . . aliī	= some . . others	bene	= well

Hostis is an official enemy, the ones your side is fighting against. Inimicus (a non-amicus) is, usually, a private enemy and might be someone on your own side.

OTHER EXERCISES

Exercise 23 H   Translate, changing it where necessary.

Dear father,

I hope you are well. I am. Our camp has been pitched near a big river. There are lots of fish in it and lots of deer in the mountains. We have huge dinners!

A new laticlavian tribune has been sent to this legion. I don't like him. All Roman senators and senators' sons are proud. They despise not only the allies but even their own citizens. The first night after* he arrived, he insulted the Gauls. We Gauls are braver than the Romans. I shall soon demonstrate this fact to him.

Love from Quintus.

* *conjunction*

Exercise 23 I   Military Puzzle.

quattuor Persae pugnant tam bene quam quinque Aegyptii. duo Graeci pugnant tam bene quam unus Persa et duo Aegyptii. qui vincent si duo Graeci et tres Aegyptii pugnant cum uno Aegyptio et quattuor Persis?

EXTRA VOCABULARY 23

glōria	= glory	nūdus	= bare
flamma	= flame	similis	= like
villa	= country house	necesse	= necessary
victōria	= victory	despērō (1)	= I despair
captīvus	= captive	excitō (1)	= I wake up
barbarus	= barbarian	vīsitō (1)	= I visit
lūdus	= game, school	līberō (1)	= I set free
numerus	= number	vexō (1)	= I annoy
silentium	= silence	valeō (2)	= I am well
parens	= parent	ascendō (3)	= I ascend
senātor	= senator	descendō (3)	= I descend
falsus	= false	resistō (3)	= I resist

CHAPTER 24

THE BATTLE AT MONS GRAUPIUS

MARCUS PATRI S.D.P.

si vales, bene est. ego valeo. pugna maxima fuit. hostes, dis gratia, vicimus.

per silvas multos dies contendebamus. tandem ad montem magnum qui Mons Graupius appellatur venimus, in quo plus quam triginta milia hostium instructi erant. ante pugnam Calgacus, Britannorum princeps, 5 orationem habuit. verba eius postea ex captivis audivimus.

'hodie tota Britannia nos spectat. hodie libertatem non modo nostram sed omnium Britannorum defendimus. ultra enim nulla est terra, nullum est mare. etiam mare Romani nunc tenent. hic est terminus Britanniae. hic est locus ubi liberos uxoresque defendemus. 10

Romani sunt raptores orbis. omnes terras, omnia maria occupare cupiunt. occidere et rapere imperium appellant et ubi solitudinem faciunt, pacem appellant.

Brigantes femina duce Romanos vicerunt. num nos viri a Romanis vincemur? Brigantes libertatem suam reciperare temptabant. nos 15 libertatem nostram numquam amisimus. nos numquam superati sumus, numquam victi. hodie demonstrabimus quos viros Caledonia pepererit.'

hanc orationem barbari cantu et clamoribus acceperunt. interea Agricola milites suos convocavit atque haec verba dixit:

'septimus annus est, milites, ex quo virtute vestra Britanniam vicistis. 20 nunc ad finem Britanniae venimus. nihil ultra est. regiones de quibus ceteri Romani non audiverunt, nos oculis videmus atque armis tenemus. ab nobis Britannia et inventa est et superata.

ego saepe in itinere, ubi per montes et flumina contendebamus, voces vestras audiebam 'quando nobis hostis dabitur? quando pugnabimus?' 25 hodie pugnabimus. hodie nobis hostis datur. nec hi sunt fortissimi Britannorum. ubi venatores animalia per silvas agitant, acerrima animalia contra venatores ruunt et pereunt, ignava fugiunt. sic acerrimi Britannorum iam ceciderunt, relictus est numerus ignavorum qui facile superabuntur. hodie erit nobis pulchra et magna victoria.' 30

oratio = speech	recipero = I get back
ultra = beyond	amitto = I lose
liberi = children	pepererit = has produced
raptor = robber	convoco = I call together
orbis (orbis, M) = world	finis = end
occupo = I seize	regio = region
imperium = empire	venator = hunter
solitudo = desert	agito = I drive
Brigantes—north British tribe who apparently helped Boadicea	pereo = I perish
	ignavus = cowardly
vir = man	

milites, ubi haec verba audiverunt, etiam acriores ad arma cucurrerunt. auxilia peditum, quae octo milia erant, in media acie, tria milia equitum in cornibus, legiones post auxilia instructae sunt. Agricola ipse ante auxilia stetit.

primo Britanni rem bene gerebant magnamque vim telorum in copias 35 nostras coniciebant. inde Agricola duas cohortes Batavorum et Tungrorum impetum facere iussit. mox hostes repellebantur. interea Britanni qui in monte instructi erant descendebant et circum terga Romanorum procedebant. Agricola tamen quattuor equitum alas contra eos misit. hostes fortiter pugnaverunt sed tandem terga verterunt et in 40 silvas montesque fugerunt. nox finis pugnae fuit. decem milia hostium occisa sunt; militum nostrorum trecenti sexaginta ceciderunt.

ipse non magna pars harum rerum fui. ubi barbari salutem fuga petiverunt, duos occidi, tres cepi. postea Agricola classem circum Britanniam navigare et terrorem Britannis inicere iussit. vale.   45

auxilia = allied forces   ala = wing (of cavalry)
pedes (peditis) = footsoldier   verto = I turn
acies = (battle) line   salus (salutis) = safety
cornu = wing (of line)   fuga = flight
ipse = (him)self   classis = fleet
cohors = cohort   inicio = I strike

The position of Mons Graupius is not known. This account of the battle and of the speeches before it is adapted from the Roman historian Tacitus. Agricola was his father-in-law.

THE LIFE OF THE LEGIONARY SOLDIER

New recruits swore an oath of loyalty to the Emperor and this was renewed every New Year's Day. Legionaries were citizens but their wives were not recognized by the state. If a wife wished to follow her husband to a new posting, she did so as best she could.

Training was tough. The recruit was taught how to march, to ride, to build camps. There was drill twice a day and three 18 mile marches a month. For weapon training he used a sword and shield of double weight. Discipline was strict; the centurion had a VITIS (vinewood staff) to 'encourage' his men.

The soldier's arms, clothing and food were supplied by the state but the cost was deducted from what he earned. The standard-bearer looked after his pay and his savings. He was off duty at sunset if not before. Near permanent camps thermae were built and soon towns grew. Near temporary camps tabernae sprang up. As well as women and children a multitude of traders followed the army.

Eight men formed a CONTUBERNIUM and shared a tent or barrack room. They also shared a mule to carry the tent and a millstone for grinding corn. Soldiers who held special posts or learnt a trade (blacksmiths, fletchers, orderlies and so on) were IMMUNES, that is free from fatigues. Better still was promotion to posts which earned increased pay. A tesserarius was paid half as much again; the signifer and optio received double pay.

After 25 years the soldier retired with a gratuity of money or land.

24 B   AN ABSENT-MINDED POET

Polymathes, ludi magister, fratrem habet, nomine Petenum, qui in casa parva prope Ostiam habitat. Petenus est poeta et vir sapiens sed valde immemor.

olim, ubi ad cenam a patrono vocatus est, in lecto recubuit sed cenae immemor dormivit. alias, ubi solus cenabat, vinum non in poculum sed 5
in cibum infudit. alias, ubi carmen scribebat, digitum, non calamum, in atramentum demisit. alias, ubi in thermas venit, tunicam suam in piscinam coniecit, ipse in apodyterio nudus recubuit.

alias, antequam in urbem cibum emptum discessit, haec verba in ianua scripsit: 'Petenus abest'. postquam cibum emit, ad casam revenit. 10
subito verba quae in ianua scripta erant conspexit. attonitus exclamavit: 'quid est hoc? Petenus abest. quam longum iter frustra feci!' magnopere iratus urbem repetivit. ibi amicus eum conspexit et 'salve' inquit. 'cur tam iratus es?' 'iratus sum,' respondit 'quod iter longum ad casam Peteni feci sed Petenus abest.' amicus rem veram suspicatus 'bono es 15
animo' inquit, 'mi amice, et casam repete. nam si semel Peteni casam intraveris, Petenum intus invenies.'

casa = cottage	*infundo = I pour*
poeta = poet	*digitus = finger*
valde = very	*calamus = pen*
immemor = forgetful	*atramentum = ink*
patronus = patron (who looked after	*demitto = I dip*
a freedman, poor man or	*antequam = before*
foreigner)	*repeto = I go again to*
recumbo = I lie down	*suspicatus = suspecting*
alias = at another time	*bono es animo = Cheer up*
poculum = cup	*intus = inside*

VOCABULARY 24

occupō (1)	= I seize	poēta (M)	= poet
convocō (1)	= I call together	fuga	= flight
vertō (3)	= I turn	līberī	= children
pereō (eo)	= I perish	vir	= man
pedes (peditis, M)	= footsoldier	cornū	= { horn
salūs (salūtis, F)	= safety		{ wing (of army)
cohors (cohortis, F)	= cohort	aciēs (5)	= line
regiō (regiōnis, F)	= region	ignāvus	= { lazy
classis (classis, F)	= fleet		{ cowardly
fīnis (fīnis, M)	= end	ipse	= self
fīnēs (plur.)	= territories	antequam	= before
orātiō (orātiōnis, F)	= speech		

PASSIVES COMPLETED (FUT. & FUT. PERF.)

In this chapter you meet the Future and Future Perfect Passive (Grammar pages 21 and 23). The Future is formed from the first principal part; the Future Perfect is formed from the last principal part.

FORMATION OF TENSES

You have now learnt all the tenses, both active and passive. There is a chart at the bottom of page 15 in the Grammar showing which principal part is used to form each tense.

Exercise 24 C   *(Mostly fut. and fut.perf. pass.)*

1. servati erunt.
2. urbs occupabitur.
3. apertum erit.
4. visus ero.
5. non audieris.
6. vincemur.
7. opus confectum erit.
8. delectatae erunt.
9. terga verterunt.
10. vulnerabimini.
11. He will have been blamed.
12. You will be asked.
13. We shall have been killed.
14. She will have been seen.
15. It will have been done.
16. The table will be moved.
17. He knows.
18. He is called Marcus.
19. It will be decided soon.
20. He drew up the line.

Exercise 24 D

1. In a smaller fleet.
2. In a very small fleet.
3. They are worse boys.
4. They are very bad boys.
5. He has more cohorts.
6. I see very many cohorts.
7. In a better region.
8. In a very good region.
9. Leader of bigger forces.
10. King of very big lands.

Exercise 24 E

1. id carmen a poeta pessimo scriptum est.
2. equites dextro cornu instruentur.
3. nonne hoc vinum est melius quam illud?
4. gratias maximas dis agere debemus.
5. a Polymathe, viro sapientissimo, docebimur.
6. quando revenies, fili carissime?
7. cives ignavi fuga salutem petiverunt.
8. verba quae dixisti ab uxore mea audita erunt.
9. Lacedaemonii plures pedites habebant quam nos.
10. ab rege et regina libenter accipieris.

Exercise 24 F

1. He is a very good poet.
2. Marcus has a better plan.
3. Very many footsoldiers fled.
4. We sailed in a smaller ship.
5. We have better soldiers than the Gauls (do).
6. We have better soldiers than sailors.
7. The wings of our line have not been drawn up.
8. Surely you have not seen a larger city than Rome?
9. The biggest boys were worse than the smallest girls.
10. The worst boy was better than the best girl.

OTHER EXERCISES

Exercise 24 G   Questions about 24 A, lines 24–34.
1. Give an English word derived from:— voces (24), hostis (25), tria (32).
2. In what case is:— flumina (24), venatores (28)?
3. Put into the present:— ceciderunt (29), dabitur (25).
4. Pick out a comparative and a superlative.
5. To whom do the pronouns refer:— ego (24), nobis (25), hi (26), qui (29)?
6. Give present infinitive of:— stetit (34), erit (30).

Exercise 24 H   Say which of the following verbs are passive. Translate them all.

1. terrentur.
2. occupabitur.
3. superabis.
4. vertent.
5. ostendetur.

6. convocati sunt.
7. iusserat.
8. culpamur.
9. delectaberis.
10. discesseris.

Exercise 24 I   Puzzle

The Roman system of weights was based on the LIBRA (=pound), equivalent to 0.72 of our pounds or 327.5 grammes. From it we get our abbreviation for pound: lb.

Can you solve the following puzzle?

Publius, agricolae filius, ad urbem cum cane iter facit. anserem quinquaginta librarum et saccum frumenti centum librarum vendere cupit. (ipse est centum librarum pondo et canis est quinquaginta librarum.)

mox ad flumen venit; pons tamen fractus est. cymba adest sed periculosum est plus quam ducentas libras in ea ponere. si canem cum ansere reliquerit, canis anserem consumet. si anserem cum frumento reliquerit, anser frumentum consumet. quid faciet puer sapiens?

VOCABULARY

Note: Numerals are not given nor words whose meaning is given beneath nor are all proper nouns. Declensions (1, 2, 3, 4, 5) are shown, and genders (*m, f, n, c*). Genitives of Third Declension nouns are given. Conjugations of verbs are shown (1, 2, 3, 3½, 4, irreg.) and the principal parts if not regular, though not all necessarily. The declension of adjectives is shown by giving the example in the Grammar, e.g. 'bonus' for 'altus'. Cases following prepositions are given. Comparatives and superlatives are referred to the Grammar. Parts of speech are given where useful. *Adverbs, conjunctions and prepositions do not decline.*

A

a *(prep + abl)*: by, from.
ab *(prep = abl)*: by, from.
abhinc: ago.
Abilēnis, -ēnis (3): Abilenis.
absum (sum): I am absent.
absurdus (bonus): absurd.
accipiō, accipere, accēpī, acceptum (3½): I receive.
ācer (acer): keen, fierce.
aciēs (5, F): battle line.
ad *(prep + acc)*: to.
addō, addere, addidī, additum (3): I add.
addūcō, addūcere, addūxī, adductum (3): I bring.
adeō: so.
adsum (sum): I am present.
adveniō (venio): I arrive.
aedificō (1): I build.
aeger (niger): ill.
Aegyptius (2, *m*): Egyptian
Aegyptus (2, *f*): Egypt.
Aemilia (1, *f*): Aemilia.
Aesōpus (2, *m*): Aesop.
aestās, aestātis (3, *f*): summer.
aetās, aetātis (3, *f*): age.
Afer (2, *m* magister): African.
Africa (1, *f*): Africa.
Africus (bonus): African.
ager (2, *m*, magister): field.
agilis (tristis): agile.
agitō (1): I hunt.
agō, agere, ēgī, āctum (3): I do, give (thanks).
agricola (1, *m*): farmer.
Agricola (1, *m*): Agricola.

Agrippa (1, *m*): Agrippa.
Albātus: White (team).
Alexander (2, *m*): Alexander.
aliī. .aliī: some. .others.
aliquid: something.
aliquis: someone.
alius: other, another.
Allia (1, *f*): Allia.
alligō (1): I tie, bind.
Alpēs: the Alps.
altus (bonus): high, deep.
ambulō (1): I walk.
amīca (1, *f*): friend
amīcus (2, *m*): friend.
amō (1): I love, like.
amphitheātrum (2, *n*): amphitheatre.
ancilla (1, *f*): slave-girl.
angustus (bonus): narrow.
animal, animālis (3, *n*): animal.
animō (**Es bonō animō**): Cheer up.
annus (2, *m*): year.
anser, anseris (3, *m*): goose.
ante *(prep + acc)*: before.
anteā *(adverb)*: before.
antequam *(conj)*: before.
anxius (bonus): anxious
aperiō, aperīre, aperuī, apertum (4): I open.
apodytērium: changing-room.
Apollō, Apollinis (3, *m*): Apollo.
appāreō (2): I appear.
appellō (1): I name
Appius (2, *m*): Appius.
appropinquō (1): I approach.

apud *(prep + acc)*: at the house of, with.
aqua (1, *f*): water.
aquaeductus (4, *m*): aqueduct.
arānea (1, *f*): spider.
arbor, arboris (3, *f*): tree.
Arcadius (2, *m*): Arcadius.
ārea (1, *f*): (court) yard.
arma (2, *n*, plur): arms.
ars, artis (3, *f*): art.
ascendō (3): I climb (on).
Athēnae (1, *f*, plur): Athens.
Athēniensis (3, *m*): Athenian.
atque: and.
ātrium (2, *n*): hall.
attonitus (bonus): astonished.
audāx, audācis (felix): bold.
audiō (4): I hear, listen (to).
Aulus (2, *m*): Aulus.
aura (1, *f*): air, breeze.
aureus (bonus): golden.
aurīga (1, *m*): charioteer.
aut: either, or.
auxilia (2, *n*, plur): allied forces.
auxilium (2, *n*): help.
avus (2, *m*): grandfather.

B

barba (1, *f*): beard.
barbarus (2, *m*): barbarian.
Bassus (2, *m*): Bassus.
Batāvi (2, *m*, plur): the Batavi.
bellum (2, *n*): war.
bene *(adverb)*: well.
benignē *(adv)*: kindly.
benignus (bonus): kind.
bēstia (1, *f*): beast.
bibō, bibere, bibī (3): I drink.
Blaesus (2, *m*): Blaesus.
Bodotria (1, *f*): Forth.
bonus (bonus): good.
  bona (*n*, plur): goods.
  Bonō es animō: Cheer up.
brevis (tristis): short.
Brigantes (3, *m*, plur): the Brigantes (tribe).
Britannia (1, *f*): Britain.
Britannus (2, *m*): Briton.

Brūtus (2, *m*): Brutus.
bulla (1, *f*): lucky charm.

C

cadō, cadere, cecidī, cāsum (3): I fall.
Caesar, Caesaris (3, *m*): Caesar.
caldārium (2, *n*): hot room.
Calēdonia (1, *f*): Scotland.
Calēdonius (2, *m*): Scotsman.
Calgacus (2, *m*): Calgacus.
calidus (bonus): hot.
callidus (bonus): clever.
Calpurnia (1, *f*): Calpurnia.
campus (2, *m*): plain.
candēlābrum (2, *n*): lampstand.
Canidia (1, *f*): Canidia.
canis, canis (3, *m*): dog.
cantō (1): I sing.
cantor, cantōris (3, *m*): singer.
cantus (4, *m*): singing.
capillus (2, *m*): hair.
capiō, capere, cēpī, captum (3½): I take, capture, adopt.
capitālis: capital.
Capitōlium (2, *n*): Capitol.
captīvitās, captīvitātis (3, *f*): captivity.
captīvus (2, *m*): prisoner.
caput, capitis (3, *n*): head.
carmen, carminis (3, *n*): song.
cārus (bonus): dear.
casa (1, *f*): cottage.
castra (2, *n*, plur): camp.
cataracta (1, *f*): waterfall.
caupō, caupōnis (3, *m*): innkeeper.
caupōna (1, *f*): inn.
causa (1, *f*): cause, reason.
caverna (1, *f*): cavern.
cecidī: *see 'cado'.*
cēlātus (bonus): hidden.
celebrō (1): I celebrate.
celeriter: quickly.
cella (1, *f*): storeroom.
cēlō (1): I hide.
cēna (1, *f*): dinner, meal.
cēnāculum (2, *n*): flat.

cēnō (1): I dine, sup.

cēpī: *see 'capio'.*

cervus (2, *m*): deer.

cēterus (bonus): the rest (of).

Christiānus (bonus): Christian.

Chrȳsērus (2, *m*): Chryserus.

cibus (2, *m*): food.

circum *(prep + acc)*: round, around.

circumspectō (1): I look round.

cistella (1, *f*): box.

cīvis, cīvis (3, *c*): citizen.

clāmō (1): I shout, cry.

clāmor, clāmōris (3, *m*): shout, shouting.

clangor, clangōris (3, *m*): noise, clanging.

clārus (bonus): clear, famous.

classis, classis (3, *f*): fleet.

claudō, claudere, clausī, clausum (3): I shut.

claudus (bonus): lame.

cōgitō (1): I think.

cohors, cohortis (3, *f*): cohort (of soldiers).

comitō (1): I accompany.

commendō (1): I commend, recommend.

comprehendō, -dere, -dī, comprehensum (3): I arrest.

condemnō (1): I condemn.

condūcō (duco): I rent.

cōnficiō, cōnficere, cōnfēcī, cōnfectum (3½): I finish.

cōniciō, cōnicere, cōniecī, cōniectum (3½): I throw.

cōnsilium (2, *n*): plan.

cōnsistō, cōnsistere, cōnstitī, cōnstitum (3): I halt.

cōnspiciō, cōnspicere, cōnspexī, cōnspectum (3½): I see.

cōnstituō, cōnstituere, cōnstituī, cōnstitūtum (3): I decide.

cōnsul, cōnsulis (3, *m*): consul.

cōnsūmō, cōnsūmere, cōnsūmpsī, cōnsūmptum (3): I eat, consume.

contendō, contendere, contendī, contentum (3): I hurry, march.

contrā *(prep + acc)*: against.

convalescō, -ere, convaluī (3): I get better.

convocō (1): I call together.

cōpia (1, *f*): quantity, plenty.

cōpiae (1, *f*, plur): forces.

coquus (2, *m*): cook.

cornū (4, *n*): horn, wing (of army).

corpus, corporis (3, *n*): body.

cōtidiē: every day.

crās: tomorrow.

crēber (niger): frequent.

crēdō, -ere, crēdidī, crēditum (3): I believe, trust.

creō (1): I elect, appoint.

crepitus (4, *m*): crackling.

crocodīlus (2, *m*): crocodile.

crūdēlissimus: very cruel.

cubiculum (2, *n*): bedroom.

cubīle, cubīlis (3, *n*): bed.

cucurrī: *see 'curro'.*

cui: *part of 'qui'.*

culīna (1, *f*): kitchen.

culpō (1): I blame.

cum *(prep + abl)*: with.

cupiō, cupere, cupīvī, cupītum (3½): I want, desire.

cūr: why.

currō, currere, cucurrī, cursum (3): I run.

currus (4, *m*): chariot.

Curtius (2, *m*): Curtius.

custōdiō (4): I guard.

custōs, custōdis (3, *m*): guard.

cymba (1, *f*): boat.

D

dē *(prep + abl)*: about, down from.

dēbeō (2): I ought, owe.

Decius (2, *m*): Decius.

decorō (1): I decorate.

dedī: *see 'do, dare, dedi'.*

dēfendō, dēfendere, dēfendī, dēfensum (3): I defend.

dēlectō (1): I please, delight.
dēmonstrō (1): I point out, show.
dens, dentis (3, *m*): tooth.
dēpōnō, dēpōnere, dēposuī, dēpositum (3): I put down.
descendō, descendere, descendī (3): I go down.
dēsiliō, dēsilīre, dēsiluī (4): I jump down.
dēsistō (3): I stop.
despērō (1): I despair.
deus (2, *m*, irreg): god.
dēvorō (1): I devour.
dexter (niger): right.
dīcō, dīcere, dīxī, dictum (3): I say, tell.
diēs (5, *m*): day.
diēs nātālis: birthday.
difficilis (tristis): difficult.
digitus (2, *m*): finger.
dīligenter: carefully.
dīmittō (3): I let go.
dīs: *part of 'deus'.*
discēdō, discēdere, discessī, discessum (3): I go, depart.
disciplīna (1, *f*): discipline.
discipulus (2, *m*): pupil.
distribuō (3): I distribute.
diu: for a long time.
diutius: longer.
dīvidō, dīvidere, dīvīsī, dīvīsum (3): I divide.
dō, dare, dedī, datum (1): I give.
doceō, docēre, docuī, doctum (2): I teach.
dominus (2, *m*): master, owner.
domus (4, *f*): home, house.
dōnum (2, *n*): gift.
dormiō (4): I sleep.
Druidae (1, *m*, plur.): Druids.
dubitō (1): I doubt, hesitate.
dubius: doubt(ful).
Dubris, Dubris (3, *f*): Dover.
dūcō, dūcere, dūxī, ductum (3), I lead, take.
dum: while.
dūrus (bonus): hard.
dux, ducis (3, *c*): leader.

E

ē *(prep + abl)*: out of, from.
eam, eās: *see 'is'.*
eārum: of them, their.
Eborācum (2, *n*): York.
ēbrius (bonus): drunk.
ecce!: look!, here is!
ēdūcō, ēdūcere, ēdūxī, ēductum (3): I lead out.
effugiō (3½): I escape.
egi: *see 'ago, agere, egī'.*
ego: I.
ēheu!: alas!
ēius: his, her.
emō, emere, ēmī, ēmptum (3): I buy.
enim: for.
eōrum: their, of them.
eōs: them.
Epimelēs (3, *m*): Epimeles.
epistola (1, *f*): letter.
eques, equitis (3, *m*): rider, horseman, knight.
equitō (1): I ride.
equus (2, *m*): horse.
eram, erō: *parts of 'sum'.*
et: *and.*
et . . et . .: both . . and . .
etiam: also, even.
eum: *part of 'is'.*
ēvānescō (3): I disappear.
ex *(prep + abl):* out of, from.
excellentissimus (bonus): most excellent.
excitō (1): I wake, rouse.
exclāmō (1): I exclaim.
exerceō (2): I exercise.
exercitus (4, *m*): army.
exit: goes out.
expedītiō, expedītiōnis (3, *f*): expedition.
expellō, expellere, expulī, expulsum (3): I drive out.
expergiscitur: wakes up.
explicō (1): I explain.
exspectō (1): I wait for.
exstinguō, -ere, exstinxī, exstinctum (3): I extinguish.
extricō (1): I disentangle.

F

fābula (1, *f*): story.
facile: easily; *or part of:*
facilis (tristis): easy.
faciō, facere, fēcī, factum (3½): I
   do, make.
falsus (bonus): false.
famēs, famis (3, *f*): hunger.
familia (1, *f*): household.
febris, febris (3, *f*): fever.
fēcī: *see 'facio'.*
fēlēs, fēlis (3, *f*): cat.
fēlīciter!: good luck!
fēlīx, fēlīcis: lucky, fortunate,
   happy.
fēmina (1, *f*): woman.
fenestra (1, *f*): window.
ferōciter: fiercely.
ferōx, ferōcis: fierce.
ferrum (2, *n*): iron.
fessus (bonus): tired.
festīnō (1): I hurry.
fīgō, fīgere, fīxī, fīxum (3): I
   fix.
fīlia (1, *f*): daughter.
fīlius (2, *m*): son.
fīnis, fīnis (3, *m*): end.
   fīnēs (plur): territories.
flamma (1, *f*): flame.
Flāvia (1, *f*): Flavia.
Flāvius (2, *m*): Flavius.
fleō, flēre, flēvī, flētum (2): I
   weep.
flōs, flōris (3, *m*): flower.
flūmen, flūminis (3, *n*): river.
fluō (3): I flow.
fortasse: perhaps.
fortis (tristis): brave.
fortiter: bravely.
fortūna (1, *f*): fortune.
forum (2, *n*): marketplace.
fossa (1, *f*): ditch.
frāctus (bonus): broken.
**frangō, frangere, frēgī,
   frāctum** (3): I break.
frāter, frātris (3, *m*): brother.
frīgidārium (2, *n*): coldroom.
frīgidus (bonus): cold.
frons, frontis (3, *f*): front.
frūmentum (2, *n*): corn.
frūstrā: in vain.
fuga (1, *f*): flight.
fugiō, fugere, fūgī (3½): I flee.
fui etc.: *parts of 'sum'.*
fūmus (2, *m*): smoke.
fūr, fūris (3, *m*): thief.

G

Gāia (1, *f*): Gaia.
Gāius (2, *m*): Gaius.
galea (1, *f*): helmet.
Gallia (1, *f*): Gaul (land).
Gallicus (bonus): Gallic.
Gallus (2, *m*): Gaul (man).
gaudium (2, *n*): joy.
geminus (bonus): twin.
gena (1, *f*): cheek.
gens, gentis (3, *f*): tribe.
genū (4, *n*): knee.
Germānia (1, *f*): Germany.
Germānus (2, *m*): German.
gerō, gerere, gessī, gestum (3): I
   wear, carry (on).
Gesoriacum (2, *n*): Boulogne.
gladiātor, gladiātōris (3, *m*):
   gladiator.
gladiātōrius (bonus):
   gladiatorial.
gladius (2, *m*): sword.
globus (2, *m*): ball.
glōria (1, *f*): glory.
Glycerāidēs, Glycerāidis (3, *m*):
   Glyceraides.
gradus (4, *m*): step.
Graecia (1, *f*): Greece.
Graecus (2, *m*): Greek.
grātia (1, *f*): gratitude, thanks.
grātiās agō: I thank.
Graupius (2, *m*): Graupius.
gravis (tristis): heavy, serious.
Gullus (2, *m*): Gullus.

H

habeō (2): I have, possess.
habitō (1): I live (in).
harēna (1, *f*): sand, arena.

hasta (1, *f*): spear.
herba (1, *f*): grass, herb.
Herculēs, Herculis (3, *m*): Hercules.
heri: yesterday.
hēus!: hey!
hic *(pronoun)*: this.
hīc *(adverb)*: here.
hiems, hiemis (3, *f*): winter.
hippopotamus (2, *m*): hippopotamus.
Hispānia (1, *f*): Spain.
Hispānus (2, *m*): Spanish.
hodiē: today.
Holcus (2, *m*): Holcus.
homō, hominis (3, *c*): man.
hōra (1, *f*): hour.
horribilis: horrible.
hortus (2, *m*): garden.
hospes, hospitis (3, *c*): guest, host, friend.
hostis, hostis (3, *c*): enemy.
Hymēn: Hymen.
Hymenaeus: Hymenaeus.

I

iam: now, already.
iānua (1, *f*): door.
ibi: there.
id: *part of 'is'.*
īdōlum (2, *n*): ghost.
ientāculum (2, *n*): breakfast.
igitur: therefore.
ignāvus (bonus): lazy, cowardly.
ignis, ignis (3, *m*): fire.
ignōrō (1): I am ignorant.
ille: that, he, she, it.
immemor: forgetful.
immortālis: immortal
impatiens, impatientis (ingens): impatient.
imperātor, imperātōris (3, *m*): general.
Imperātor: Emperor.
impetus (4, *m*): attack.
in *(prep + acc or abl)*: in, on, into, on to, at.
incendium (2, *n*): fire.

incendō, incendere, incendī, incensum (3): I burn.
incursō (1): I attack.
inde: then.
indūcō (dūco): I lead in.
infirmus (bonus): weak.
infundō, infundere, infūdī, infūsum (3): I pour on.
ingēns, ingentis: huge.
ingravescō (3): I get worse.
inhabitantēs: inhabitants.
iniciō, inicere, inīecī, iniectum (3½): *throw in.*
inimīcus (2, *m*): enemy.
inmittō, inmittere, inmīsī, inmissum (3): I aim at, let in, thrust, launch.
innocens, innocentis (ingens): innocent.
innumerābilis (tristis): innumerable.
inquit: says.
insānus (bonus): mad.
inspiciō, inspicere, inspexī (3½): I look in/at, inspect.
instruo, instruere, instruxī, instructum (3): I draw up.
insula (1, *f*): island, block.
insultō (1): I insult.
intellegō, intellegere, intellēxī, intellēctum (3): I understand, realize.
intentē: intently.
inter *(prep + acc)*: among, between.
intereā: meanwhile.
interrogō (1): I interrogate.
intrō (1): I enter.
veniō, invenīre, invēnī, inventum (4): I find.
invītō (1): I invite.
iō!: o!, hurrah!, hurray!
ipse: self, himself, herself.
īra (1, *f*): anger.
īrātus (bonus): angry.
is: that, he, she, it.
ita vērō: yes.
Italia (1, *f*): Italy.
itaque: and so, therefore.

iter, itineris (3, *n*): journey, route, expedition.
iterum: again.
iubeō, iubēre, iussī, iussum (2): I order.
iūdex, iūdicis (3, *c*): judge.
iugulō (1): I cut the throat, murder.
iugulum (2, *n*): throat.
Iūlia (1, *f*): Julia.
Iūlius (2, *m*): Julius.
iungō, iungere, iunxī, iunctum (3): I join.
Iuppiter, Iovis (3, *m*): Jupiter.
iuvenis, iuvenis (3, *m*): young man.

L

labōrō (1): I work.
Lacedaemonius (2, *m*): Spartan.
lacerō (1): I tear.
laetus (bonus): happy.
Laevīnus (2, *m*): Laevinus.
Lamachus (2, *m*): Lamachus.
lanterna (1, *f*): lantern.
lāticlāvius (bonus): with a broad purple band.
laudō (1): I praise.
laurus (2, *f*): bay, laurel.
lectus (2, *m*): bed, couch.
legiō, legiōnis (3, *f*): legion.
legō, legere, lēgī, lēctum (3): I read, choose.
lentē: slowly.
leō, leōnis (3, *m*): lion.
libenter: gladly.
liber (2, *m*, magister): book, bark (of tree).
līberī (2, *m*, plur): children.
līberō (1): I set free.
libertās, lībertātis (3, *f*): freedom.
lībertus (2, *m*): freedman.
lībra (1, *f*): pound.
licet: it is allowed.
Lindum (2, *n*): Lincoln.
lītus, lītoris (3, *n*): shore.
locus (2, *m*): place.

Londinium (2, *n*): London.
longus (bonus): long.
lōrīca (1, *f*): breastplate.
Lūcius (2, *m*): Lucius.
lūdō, lūdere, lūsī, lūsum (3): I play.
lūdus (2, *m*): school, game.
lupus (2, *m*): wolf.
Lutetius (2, *m*): Lutetius.
lux, lūcis (3, *f*): light.
lyra (1, *f*): lyre.

M

Macedō, Macedonis (3, *m*): Macedonian.
madidus (bonus): wet.
maestus (bonus): sad.
magicus (bonus): magic.
magister (2, *m*): master.
magistrātus (4, *m*): magistrate.
magnopere: very much.
magnus (bonus): big, great.
maior: *see grammar page 10.*
malus (bonus): bad.
maneō, manēre, mansī, mansum (2): I remain, stay.
manus (4, *f*): hand.
Marcus (2, *m*): Marcus.
mare, maris (3, *n*): sea.
marītus (2, *m*): husband.
māter, mātris (3, *f*): mother.
mātrimōnium (2, *n*): marriage.
maximus (bonus): very big.
medicāmentum (2, *n*): medicine.
medicus (2, *m*): doctor.
medius (bonus): middle.
melior, meliōris: better.
Melissa (1, *f*): Melissa.
Menoetēs (3, *m*): Menoetes.
mēnsa (1, *f*): table.
mercātor, mercātōris (3, *m*): merchant.
merīdiēs (5, *m*): noon.
mēta (1, *f*): turning point.
meus (bonus): my.
mīles, mīlitis (3, *m*): soldier.
minimē: no.

minimus: *see grammar page 10.*
mīrus (bonus): amazing.
miser (tener): wretched.
missiō, missiōnis (3, *f*): release.
mittō, mittere, mīsī, missum
  (3): I send.
mixtus (bonus): mixed.
modo: only, just.
Mona (1, *f*): Anglesey.
moneō (2): I advise, warn.
mons, montis (3, *m*): mountain.
mora (1, *f*): delay.
morbus (2, *m*): disease.
mors, mortis (3, *f*): death.
mortālis: mortal.
mortuus (bonus): dead.
moveō, movēre, mōvī, mōtum
  (2): I move.
mox: soon.
mulceō (2): I soothe.
multus (bonus): much, many.
mūlus (2, *m*): mule.
mundus (bonus): clean.
mūniō (4): I fortify.
mūrus (2, *m*): wall.
mustāceus (2, *m*): wedding cake.
myrtus (2, *f*): myrtle.

N

nam: for.
Narbarsēs, Narbarsis (3, *m*):
  Narbarses.
nārrō (1): I tell.
nātālis (dies): birthday.
natō (1): I swim.
nātus (bonus): old, born.
nauta (1, *m*): sailor.
nāvigō (1): I sail.
nāvis, nāvis (3, *f*): ship.
-ne: ?
nec: neither, nor.
necesse: necessary.
necō (1): I kill.
neglegēns (ingēns): careless.
nēmō: no one.
nesciō (4): I do not know.
Nīcerus (2, *m*): Nicerus.
niger: black.

nihil *(indecl):* nothing.
nisi: unless, if not.
nōbīs: *part of 'ego'.*
nōmen, nōminis (3, *n*): name.
nōn: not.
nōndum: not yet.
nōnne: surely.
nōs; we, us.
noster (niger): our.
nōveram: I knew.
novus (bonus): new.
nox, noctis (3, *f*): night.
nūbēs, nūbis (3, *f*): cloud.
nūdus (bonus): bare.
nūllus (unus): no.
num?: surely not?
numerus (2, *m*): number.
numquam: never.
nunc: now.
nūntiō (1): I announce.
nūntius (2, *m*): message,
  messenger.
nuptiae (1, *f*, plur): wedding.
nuptiālis (tristis): wedding *(adj).*

O

Ō: O.
obscūrus (bonus): dark.
occīdō, occīdere, occīdī,
  occīsum (3): I kill.
occupo (1): I seize.
oculus (2, *m*): eye.
ōlim: once.
omnis (tristis): all.
onus, oneris (3, *n*); burden.
oppidum (2, *n*): town.
oppugnō (1): I attack.
optimus (bonus): very good.
opus, operis (3, *n*): work.
orātiō, orātiōnis (3, *f*): speech.
Ordovices: the Ordovices.
ornō (1): I decorate, adorn.
Orphēus (2, *m*): Orpheus.
ōs, ōris (3, *n*): face, mouth.
ostendō, ostendere, ostendī,
  ostentum (3): I show.
Ostia (1, *f*): Ostia.
ōtiōsus (bonus): idle.

P

paedagōgus (2, *m*): tutor.
paene: almost.
palaestra (1, *f*): exercise ground.
panthēra (1, *f*): panther.
parens, parentis (3, *c*): parent.
parō (1): I prepare.
pars, partis (3, *f*): part.
parvus (bonus): small.
pater, patris (3, *m*): father.
paucus (bonus): few.
paullō: little.
pāx, pācis (3, *f*): peace.
pectus, pectoris (3, *n*): chest, breast.
pecūnia (1, *f*): money.
pedes, peditis (3, *m*): foot-soldier.
pēior: *see grammar page 10.*
per *(prep + acc)*: through, along.
pereō, perīre, periī: I perish.
perīculōsus (bonus): dangerous.
perīculum (2, *n*): danger.
peristȳlium (2, *n*): court-yard.
Persa (1, *m*): Persian.
pēs, pedis (3, *m*): foot.
pessimus: *grammar page 10.*
Petēnus (2, *m*): Petenus.
petō, petere, petīvī, petītum (3): I seek, attack, make for.
Phaedrus (2, *m*): Phaedrus.
Pharaōnēs: the Pharaohs.
Philerastus (2, *m*): Philerastus.
pictura (1, *f*): picture.
pīlum (2, *n*): spear.
piscīna (1, *f*): swimming pool.
plaustrum (2, *n*): waggon.
plēnus (bonus): full.
plūrēs: *grammar page 9.*
plūrimus: very many, most.
plūs: *grammar pages 9, 10*
pōculum (2, *n*): cup.
poēta (1, *m*): poet.
Polymathēs, Polymathis (3, *m*): Polymathes.
pondō: in weight.
pōnō, pōnere, posuī, positum (3): I place, put, pitch.

pons, pontis (3, *m*): bridge.
Pons: Bridge.
populus (2, *m*): people.
porta (1, *f*): gate.
porticus (4, *f*): portico.
portō (1): I carry.
portus (4, *m*): port.
post *(prep + acc)*: after, behind.
posteā: afterwards.
postis, postis (3, *m*): post.
postquam *(conj)*: after.
postrīdiē: the next day.
Postumus (2, *m*): Postumus.
praecipitō (1): I fall head-long.
praeclārus (bonus): famous.
praeda (1, *f*): booty, plunder.
praefectus (2, *m*): commander.
praemium (2, *n*): reward.
prandium (2, *n*): lunch.
Prasinus (2, *m*): Green.
prīma lux: dawn.
prīmō: at first.
princeps, principis (3, *c*): chief.
prōcēdō, prōcēdere, prōcessī, prōcessum (3): I proceed.
procul: far (away).
prope *(prep + acc; or adv)*: near.
proximus (bonus): next, last, very near.
pūblicus (bonus): public.
Publius (2, *m*): Publius.
puella (1, *f*): girl.
puer (2, *m*): boy.
pūgiō, pūgiōnis (3, *m*): dagger.
pugna (1, *f*): fight.
pugnō (1): I fight.
pulcher (niger): beautiful.
pulsō (1): I hit, knock.
pūrus (bonus): pure.
puteus (2, *m*): well.

Q

quadrīga (1, *f*): four-horse chariot.
quae: *part of 'qui'.*
quaerō (3): I search, ask, seek.
quaestor, quaestōris (3, *m*): quaestor.

quam: how, than, as, what.
quamquam: although.
quando?: when?
Quartus (2, *m*): Quartus.
-que: and.
quī: who, which.
quid?: what?
Quintus (2, *m*): Quintus.
quis?: who?
quō?: where to?
quod: because, *or part of 'qui, quae, quod'.*
quōmodo?: how?
quoque: also.
quot?: how many?

R

rapiō, rapere, rapuī, raptum (3½): I seize.
raptō (1): I pull, seize.
rārus (bonus): rare.
recumbō, recumbere, recubuī (3): I lie down.
refrīgerō (1): I cool.
rēgīna (1, *f*): queen.
regiō, regiōnis (3, *f*): region.
regō, regere, rēxī, rēctum (3): I rule, guide, control.
relaxō (1): I relax.
relinquō, relinquere, relīquī, relictum (3): I leave.
remedium (2, *n*): remedy.
removeō, removēre, remōvī, remōtum (2): I remove.
repellō, repellere, reppulī, repulsum (3): I drive back.
rēs (5, *f*): thing, fact, matter.
resistō, resistere, restitī (3): I resist.
respondeō, -ēre, respondī, responsum (2): I reply.
responsum (2, *n*): reply.
retardō (1): I slow (up).
rēte, rētis (3, *n*): net.
rētiārius (2, *m*): netman.
reveniō, revenīre, revēnī, reventum (4): I come back.
rēx, rēgis (3, *m*): king.

rīdeō, rīdēre, rīsī, rīsum (2): I laugh, smile.
ridiculus (bonus): ridiculous.
rīpa (1, *f*): bank.
rogō (1): I ask.
Rōma (1, *f*): Rome.
Rōmānus (2, *m*): Roman.
rosa (1, *f*): rose.
rota (1, *f*): wheel.
ruō (3): I rush.
Russatus: Red (team).

S

S.D.P.: *see page 52.*
saccus (2, *m*): sack.
sacerdōs, sacerdōtis (3, *m*): priest.
sacrificium (2, *n*): sacrifice.
saepe: often.
saevus (bonus): savage.
sagitta (1, *f*): arrow.
saltō (1): I dance.
salūs, salūtis (3, *f*): safety, greetings.
salūtō (1): I greet.
salvē/salvēte: hail, hello, good morning.
salvus (bonus): safe.
sanguinolentus (bonus): blood-stained.
sanguis, sanguinis (3, *m*): blood.
sānō (1): I heal.
sapiēns (ingēns): wise.
sapiō (3½): I am wise.
satis: enough.
saxum (2, *n*): rock.
scālae (1, *f*, plur): stairs.
scapha (1, *f*): boat.
sciō (4): I know.
scrībō, scrībere, scrīpsī, scrīptum (3): I write.
scūtum (2, *n*): shield.
sē: himself, herself, itself, themselves.
secūtor (3, *m*): chaser.
sed: but.
sedeō, sedēre, sēdī, sessum (2): I sit.

semel: once.
semper: always.
senātor, senātōris (3, *m*): senator.
senex, senis (3, *m*): old man.
sentiō, sentīre, sensī, sensum (4): I notice, feel.
servitūs, servitūtis (3, *f*): slavery.
servō (1): I save, keep.
servus (2, *m*): slave.
Sextus (2, *m*): Sextus.
sī: if.
sīc: so, thus.
Sicilia (1, *f*): Sicily.
signō (1): I sign.
signum (2, *n*): sign, signal.
silentium (2, *n*): silence.
silva (1, *f*): forest, wood.
similis (tristis): like.
simplex (felix): simple.
sine *(prep + abl):* without.
singulātim: one by one.
sinister (niger): left.
sōl, sōlis (3, *m*): sun.
sōlum *(adverb):* only.
sōlus (unus): only, alone.
somnium (2, *n*): dream.
sonus (2, *m*): noise, sound.
sordidus (bonus): dirty.
soror, sorōris (3, *f*): sister.
Sparta (1, *f*): Sparta.
spectāculum (2, *n*): show.
spectātor, spectātōris (3, *m*): spectator.
spectō (1): I look (at).
spēs (5, *f*): hope.
splendidus (bonus): splendid.
st!: sh!
statim: immediately.
stīria (1, *f*): icicle.
stō, stare, stetī, statum (1): I stand.
stola (1, *f*): dress, gown.
strigilis (3, *f*): strigil.
stringō (3): I graze, draw.
stultus (bonus): stupid.
stupeō (2): I gape.
sub *(prep + abl):* under.

subitō: suddenly.
submergō, -ere, submersī, submersum (3): I submerge.
subvenī/subvenīte!: help!
sum (irreg): I am.
summus (bonus): highest, top, utmost.
sūmō, sūmere, sūmpsī, sūmptum (3): I take up, pick up.
super *(prep + acc):* over.
superbus (bonus): proud.
superō (1): I defeat.
surgō (3): I get up.
suspīciō, suspīciōnis (3, *f*): suspicion.
suus (bonus): his, her, its, their.
Syrius (bonus): Syrian.

T

tabellārius (2, *m*): letter-carrier.
taberna (1, *f*): shop, inn.
tabernāculum (2, *n*): tent.
tablīnum (2, *n*): study.
tacē!/tacēte!: shut up!
taceō (2): I am silent.
tacitus (bonus): silent.
Talassiō: Talassio.
tam: so.
tam bene quam: as well as.
tamen: however.
Tamesis, Tamesis (3, *m*): Thames.
tandem: at length, at last.
tangō, tangere, tetigī, tāctum (3): I touch.
tegō, tegere, tēxī, tēctum (3): I cover.
telum (2, *n*): spear, weapon.
tempestās, tempestātis (3, *f*): storm, weather.
templum (2, *n*): temple.
temptō (1): I try.
tempus, temporis (3, *n*): time.
teneō, tenēre, tenuī, tentum (2): I hold.
tener: soft, tender.
tepidārium (2, *n*): warm-room.

tepidus (bonus): warm.
ter: thrice, three times.
tergum (2, *n*): back.
terminus (2, *m*): end.
terra (1, *f*): land, ground.
terreō (2): I frighten.
terribilis (tristis): terrible.
territus (bonus): frightened.
terror, terrōris (3, *m*): terror.
testis, testis (3, *c*): witness.
tetigī: *see 'tango'.*
theātrum (2, *n*): theatre.
Thēbae (1, *f*, plur): Thebes.
Thēbānus (2, *m*): Theban.
Theopropidēs, Theopropidis (3, *m*): Theopropides.
thermae (1, *f*, plur): baths.
Tiberis, Tiberis (3, *m*): Tiber.
timeō (2): I fear, am afraid.
timidus (bonus): timid.
timor, timōris (3, *m*): fear.
Titūrius (2, *m*): Titurius.
toga (1, *f*): toga, cloak.
tollō (3): I lift, remove.
tōtus (unus): whole, completely.
trahō, trahere, trāxī, tractum (3): I drag, pull.
Trānio (3, *m*): Tranio.
tranquillus (bonus): calm.
transfīgō, transfīgere, transfīxī, transfīxum (3): I pierce, run through.
tribūnus (2, *m*): tribune.
trīclīnium (2, *n*): dining-room.
tridens, tridentis (3, *m*): three-pronged spear, trident.
trīstis: sad.
triumphans: triumphant.
triumphus (2, *m*): triumph.
Trōia (1, *f*): Troy.
Trōiānus (2, *m*): Trojan.
tū: you.
Tullus (2, *m*): Tullus.
Tungrī (2, *m*, plur): the Tungri.
tunica (1, *f*): tunic.
turba (1, *f*): crowd.
turbulentus (bonus): muddy.
turpis (tristis): disgraceful.

tūtus (bonus): safe.
tuus (bonus): your.

U

ubi: where, when.
ultrā: beyond.
ululō (1): I howl, scream.
unguentāria taberna: scent shop.
unguentum (2, *n*): scent.
urbs, urbis (3, *f*): city.
ursa (1, *f*): bear.
ūva (1, *f*): grape.
uxor, uxōris (3, *f*): wife.

V

valē!: goodbye!
valedīco, valedīcere, valedīxī (3): I say goodbye.
valeō (2): I am well.
  multum valet: is very good.
varius (bonus): various.
vēlōx, vēlōcis: swift.
vēnālicius (2, *m*): slave-dealer.
vēndō, vēndere, vēndidī, vēnditum (3): I sell.
venēfica (1, *f*): poisoner, witch.
venēnātus (bonus): poisoned.
venēnō (1): I poison.
Venetus (2, *m*): Blue (team).
veniō, venīre, vēnī, ventum (4): I come.
verberō (1): I whip.
verbum (2, *n*): word.
vero— ita vērō: yes.
vertō, vertere, vertī, versum (3): I turn.
vērus (bonus): true.
vester (niger): your.
vestis, vestis (3, *f*): garment; (plur): clothes.
vexō (1): I annoy.
via (1, *f*): road, street.
victor: winner, victorious.
victōria (1, *f*): victory.
videō, vidēre, vīdī, vīsum (2): I see.

vigil, vigilis (3, *m*): watch-man.
vigilia (1, *f*): watch.
vīgintīvir: magistrate.
vīlicus (2, *m*): bailiff.
villa (1, *f*): villa, country house.
vincō, vincere, vīcī, victum (3): I conquer, win.
vinculum (2, *n*): chain, bond.
vīnum (2, *n*): wine.
vīpera (1, *f*): viper.
Vipsānia (1, *f*): Vipsania.
vir (2, *m*): man.
vīrēs (plur of vis): strength.
virgō, virginis (3, *f*): maiden.
virtūs, virtūtis (3, *f*): courage, virtue.

vīs (3, *f*, irreg): force, strength.
vīsitō (1): I visit.
vīta (1, *f*): life.
vītō (1): I avoid.
vīvō, vīvere, vīxī, vīctum (3): I live.
voco (1): I call, invite.
volō (1): I fly.
vōs: you (*plural*).
vōx, vōcis (3, *f*): voice.
vulnerō (1): I wound.
vulnus, vulneris (3, *n*): wound.

Z

Zōilus (2, *m*): Zoilus.

ENGLISH—LATIN VOCABULARY

A

abandon: relinquo, -ere, reliqui, relictum (3).

about: de (*prep* + *abl*).

absent—**am absent:** absum (sum).

adopt (plan): capio, -ere, cepi, captum (3½).

advance: procedo, -ere, processi, processum (3).

advise: moneo (2).

Aemilia: Aemilia (1, *f*).

afraid— **am afraid (of):** timeo (2).

Africa: Africa (1, *f*).

African: Afer (magister, *m*).

after *prep*: post (+ *acc*)
      conj: postquam
      adv: postea.

afterwards: postea (*adv*).

again: iterum (*adverb*).

against: contra (*prep* + *acc*).

Agricola: Agricola (1, *m*).

all: omnis (tristis).

ally: socius (2, *m*).

alone: solus (unus).

along: per (*prep* + *acc*).

already: iam (*adverb*).

also: quoque, etiam (*advs*).

although: quamquam (*conj*).

always: semper (*adverb*).

am: sum (irreg).

among: inter (*prep* + *acc*).

and: et (*conjunction*).

anger: ira (1, *f*).

Anglesey: Mona (1, *f*).

angry: iratus (bonus).

announce: nuntio (1).

answer: respondeo, -ere, respondi, responsum (2).

approach: appropinquo (1).

arena: harena (1, *f*).

arms: arma (2, *n*, plur).

army: exercitus (4, *m*).

around: circum (*prep* + *acc*).

arrest: comprehendo, -ere, comprehendi, comprehensum (3)

arrive: advenio, advenire, adveni (4).

arrow: sagitta (1, *f*).

ask: rogo (1).

asleep—**am asleep:** dormio (4)

at: in (*prep* + *acc*).
  at last: tandem (*adverb*).
  at length: tandem (*adverb*).

attack *noun:* impetus (4, *m*).
      verb: oppugno (1) *or* incurso (1).

Aulus: Aulus (2, *m*).

avoid: vito (1).

B

bad: malus (bonus).

ball: globus (2, *m*).

bank: ripa (1, *f*).

battle: pugna (1, *f*).

battle-line: acies (5, *f*).

be: sum (irreg).

bear: ursa (1, *f*).

beard: barba (1, *f*).

beautiful: pulcher (niger).

bed: cubile, cubilis (3, *n*).

bedroom: cubiculum (2, *n*).

because: quod (*conj*).

before: ante (*prep* + *acc*).

between: inter (*prep* + *acc*).

big: magnus (bonus).

black: niger.

blame: culpo (1).

blood: sanguis, sanguinis (3, *m*).

body: corpus, corporis (3, *n*).

bold: audax, audacis (felix).

book: liber (2, *m*, magister).

both..and..: et..et..(*conj*)

brave: fortis (tristis).

bravely: fortiter (*adv*).

bridge: pons, pontis (3, *m*).

Britain: Britannia (1, *f*).

Briton: Britannus (2, *m*).

brother: frater, fratris (3, *m*).

build: aedifico (1).

burden: onus, oneris (3, *n*).

but: sed (*conjunction*).

buy: emo, emere, emi, emptum (3)

by: a, ab (*prep + abl*) *or abl only.*

C

call: voco (1).

camp: castra (2, *n,* plur).

Campus Martius: Campus Martius (2, *m*).

Capitol: Capitolium (2, *n*).

capture: capio, capere, cepi, captum (3½).

carry: porto (1).

carry on: gero, gerere, gessi, gestum (3).

cast: conicio, conicere, conieci, coniectum (3½).

catch: *see 'capture'.*

chain: vinculum (2, *n*).

charioteer: auriga (1, *m*).

chief: princeps, principis (3, *c*).

choose: lego, legere, legi, lectum (3).

Circus: Circus (2, *m*).

Circus Maximus: Circus Maximus (2, *m*).

citizen: civis, civis (3, *c*).

city: urbs, urbis (3, *f*).

cloak: toga (1, *f*).

clothes. *plural of* vestis, vestis (3, *f*).

cloud: nubes, nubis (3, *f*).

cohort: cohors, cohortis (3, *f*).

come: venio, venire, veni, ventum (4).

come at: peto, petere, petivi, petitum (3).

come back: revenio, -ire, reveni (4).

conquer: vinco, vincere, vici, victum (3).

consul: consul, consulis (3, *m*).

control: rego, regere, rexi, rectum (3).

courage: virtus, virtutis (3, *f*).

courtyard: peristylium (2, *n*).

cover: tego, tegere, texi, tectum (3).

crash: corruo (3).

crowd: turba (1, *f*).

cry *noun:* clamor, clamoris (*m*) *verb: weep:* fleo, flere, flevi, fletum (2), *shout.* clamo (1).

cunning: callidus (bonus).

cup: poculum (2, *n*).

D

danger: periculum (2, *n*).

daughter: filia (1, *f*).

dawn: prima lux (lucis, *f*).

day: dies (5, *m*).

dead: mortuus (bonus).

death: mors, mortis (3, *f*).

decide: constituo, -ere, constitui, constitutum (3).

decorate: decoro (1).

deep: altus (bonus).

deer: cervus (2, *m*).

defeat: supero (1).

defend: defendo, defendere, defendi, defensum (3).

delight: delecto (1).

demonstrate: demonstro (1).

depart: discedo, discedere, discessi, discessum (3).

desire: cupio, cupere, cupivi, cupitum (3½).

despise: contemno (3).

difficult: difficilis (tristis).
  with difficulty: aegre (*adverb*).

dinner: cena (1, *f*).

dirty: sordidus (bonus).

disappear: evanesco, -ere, evanui (3).

disease: morbus (2, *m*).

disgraceful: turpis (tristis).

ditch: fossa (1, *f*).

do: (=*perform*): facio, facere, feci, factum (3½). *otherwise auxiliary.*

dog: canis, canis (3, *m*).

door: ianua (1, *f*).

doubt: dubito (1).

down from: de (*prep + abl*).

drag: traho, trahere, traxi, tractum (3).

draw up: instruo, instruere, instruxi, instructum (3).
dress: stola (1, *f*).
drink: bibo, bibere, bibi (3).
drunk(en): ebrius (bonus).

E

easily: facile (*adverb*).
easy: facilis (tristis).
eat: consumo, consumere, consumpsi (3).
Emperor: Imperator, Imperatoris (3, *m*).
enemy: hostis, hostis (3, *c*).
enter: intro (1).
Epimeles: Epimeles, Epimelis (3, *m*).
even: etiam (*adverb*).
eventually: tandem (*adv*).
every day: cotidie (*adv*).
evil: scelestus (bonus).
eye: oculus (2, *m*).

F

face: os, oris (3, *n*).
fact: res (5, *f*).
fall: cado, cadere, cecidi, casum (3).
far: procul (*adverb*).
farmer: agricola (1, *m*).
father: pater, patris (3, *m*).
fear: *verb:* timeo (2).
  noun: timor, timoris (3, *m*).
few: paucus (bonus).
field: ager (2, *m*, magister).
fierce: acer *or* ferox, ferocis (felix).
fight: pugno (1).
find: invenio, invenire, inveni, inventum (4).
finish: conficio, conficere, confeci, confectum (3½).
fire: ignis, ignis (3, *m*).
fish: piscis, piscis (3, *m*).
Flavia: Flavia (1, *f*).
flee: fugio, -ere, fugi (3½).
fleet: classis, classis (3, *f*).

flower: flos, floris (3, *m*).
food: cibus (2, *m*).
foolish: stultus (bonus).
foot: pes, pedis (3, *m*).
footsoldier: pedes, peditis (3, *m*).
for: *dative or time how long.*
force: vis (3, *f*, irreg).
forces: copiae (1, *f*, plur).
forest: silva (1, *f*).
fortify: munio (4).
fortunate: felix, felicis.
forum: forum (2, *n*).
freedom: libertas, libertatis (3, *f*).
friend: amicus (2, *m*).
frighten: terreo (2).
from: a (*prep + abl*).
full: plenus (bonus).

G

Gaius: Gaius (2, *m*).
Gallic: Gallicus (bonus).
garden: hortus (2, *m*).
garment: vestis, vestis (3, *f*).
gate: porta (1, *f*).
Gaul *land:* Gallia (1, *f*).
  man: Gallus (2, *m*).
general: imperator, imperatoris (3, *m*).
German: Germanus (2, *m*).
get up: surgo (3).
ghost: idolum (2, *n*).
gift: donum (2, *n*).
girl: puella (1, *f*).
give: do, dare, dedi, datum (1).
go: discedo, discedere, discessi (3).
good: bonus.
goods: bona (2, *n*, plur).
gown: stola (1, *f*).
grandfather: avus (2, *m*).
great: magnus (bonus).
Greek: Graecus (2, *m*).
greet: saluto (1).
ground: terra (1, *f*).
guard: custos, custodis (3, *m*).
guide: rego, regere, rexi, rectum (3).

H

hair: capillus (2, *m*).
hall: atrium (2, *n*).
hand: manus (4, *f*).
happy: laetus (bonus).
harbour: portus (4, *m*).
hard: durus (bonus).
hasten: festino (1).
have = *possess:* habeo (2).
    otherwise perfect.
head: caput, capitis (3, *n*).
hear: audio (4).
heavy: gravis (tristis).
help: auxilium (2, *n*).
her: *adj:* suus (bonus).
    pron: part of 'is'.
hesitate: dubito (1).
hide: celo (1).
high: altus (bonus).
him: *part of 'is'.*
hire: conduco, conducere,
    conduxi (3).
his: *his own:* suus (bonus).
    someone else's: eius.
Holcus: Holcus (2, *m*).
hold: teneo, tenere, tenui,
    tentum (2).
home: domus (4, *fem*).
hope: spes (5, *f*).
horn: cornu (4, *n*).
horse: equus (2, *m*).
hour: hora (1, *f*).
house: domus (4, *fem*).
how: quam (*adverb*).
however: tamen (*adv*).
huge: ingens, ingentis.
hurry: festino (1).

I

I: ego.
if: si (*conjunction*).
ill: aeger (niger).
immediately: statim (*adv*).
in: in (*prep + abl*).
in vain: frustra (*adv*).
in order to: *use supine.*
innkeeper: caupo, -onis (*m*).
inspect: inspicio, -ere, inspexi,
    inspectum (3½).

insult: insulto (1).
into: in (*prep + acc*).
island: insula (1, *f*).
it: *part of 'is'.*
its: suus (bonus).

J

job: opus, operis (3, *n*).
join: iungo, iungere, iunxi,
    iunctum (3).
journey: iter, itineris (3, *n*).
judge: iudex, iudicis (3, *c*).
Julia: Iulia (1, *f*).
Jupiter: Iuppiter, Iovis (3, *m*).

K

keen: acer.
kill: neco (1); *or* occido, -ere,
    occidi, occisum (3).
kind: benignus (bonus).
kindly: benigne (*adverb*).
king: rex, regis (3, *m*).
knee: genu (4, *n*).
know: scio (4).
  not know: nescio (4).

L

land: terra (1, *f*).
large: magnus (bonus).
laticlavian: laticlavius (bonus).
laugh: rideo, ridere, risi, risum
    (2).
launch: inmitto, inmittere,
    inmisi, inmissum (3).
lead: duco, ducere, duxi, ductum
    (3).
leader: dux, ducis (3, *c*).
leave: *depart:* discedo,
    -ere, discessi (3).
    abandon: relinquo, -ere,
    reliqui, relictum (3).
left: sinister (niger).
legion: legio, legionis (3, *f*).
length—at length: tandem
    (*adverb*).
letter: epistola (1, *f*).
life: vita (1, *f*).

light: lux, lucis (3, *f*).
like: diligo, diligere, dilexi (3); *or* amo (1).
line (of battle): acies (5, *f*).
lion: leo, leonis (3, *m*).
listen (to): audio (4).
little: parvus (bonus).
live: *dwell:* habito (1);
    exist: vivo, vivere, vixi, victum (3).
long: longus (bonus).
look (at): specto (1).
look for: peto, petere, petivi, petitum (3).
look round: circumspecto (1).
lord: dominus (2, *m*).
love: amo (1).
Lucius: Lucius (2, *m*).
lucky: felix, felicis.

M

make: facio, facere, feci, factum (3½).
man: homo, hominis (3, *c*).
many: multus (bonus).
march: contendo, contendere, contendi (3).
Marcus: Marcus (2, *m*).
marketplace: forum (2, *n*).
master (school): magister (2, *m*).
    (slaves): dominus (2, *m*).
matter: res (5, *f*).
Maximus: Maximus (bonus).
me: *part of 'ego'*.
meal: cena (1, *f*).
Melissa: Melissa (1, *f*).
merchant: mercator, mercatoris (3, *m*).
messenger: nuntius (2, *m*).
midday: meridies (5, *m*).
mine: meus (bonus).
Mona: Mona (1, *f*).
money: pecunia (1, *f*).
mother: mater, matris (3, *f*).
mountain: mons, montis (3, *m*).
mouth: os, oris (3, *n*).
move: moveo, movere, movi, motum (2).
much: multus (bonus).

too much: nimis (*adverb*).
very much: magnopere (*adv*).
my: meus (bonus).

N

name: nomen, nominis (3, *n*).
near: prope (*prep + acc*).
neither: nec (*conj*).
net: rete, retis (3, *n*).
never: numquam (*adv*).
new: novus (bonus).
night: nox, noctis (3, *f*).
no *adv:* minime;
    adj: nullus (unus).
noise: sonus (2, *m*).
noon: meridies (5, m).
nor: nec (*conj*).
not: non (*adv*).
now: nunc *or* iam (*advs*).

O

O: O.
of: *use genitive*.
often: saepe (*adv*).
old man: senex, senis (3, *m*).
on: in (*prep + abl*).
  on to: in (*prep + acc*).
once: olim (*adv*).
only *adv:* modo;
    adj: solus (unus).
open: aperio, aperire, aperui, apertum (4).
order: iubeo, iubere, iussi, iussum (2).
  in order to: *use supine*.
other: ceterus (bonus).
ought: debeo (2).
our: noster (niger).
out of: e, ex (*prep + abl*).
owe: debeo (2).

P

part: pars, partis (3, *f*).
peace: pax, pacis (3, *f*).
people: populus (2, *m*).
perhaps: fortasse (*adv*).
pick up: sumo, sumere, sumpsi, sumptum (3).

pitch: pono, ponere, posui, positum (3).

place *noun:* locus (2, *m*).
      verb: pono, ponere, posui, positum (3).

plan: consilium (2, *n*).

play: ludo, ludere, lusi (3).

please: delecto (1).

poet: poeta (1, *m*).

point out: demonstro (1).

port: portus (4, *m*).

possess: habeo (2).

praise: laudo (1).

prepare: paro (1).

present: donum (2, *n*).
  am present: adsum (sum).

proceed: procedo, -ere, processi (3).

proud: superbus (bonus).

puddle: lacuna (1, *f*).

put: pono (*see 'place'*).

Q

Quartus: Quartus (2, *m*).

queen: regina (1, *f*).

quick: velox, velocis (felix).

quickly: celeriter (*adv*).

Quintus: Quintus (2, *m*).

R

read: lego, legere, legi, lectum (3).

receive: accipio, accipere, accepi, acceptum (3½).

region: regio, regionis (3, *f*).

remain: maneo, manere, mansi, mansum (2).

rent: conduco, conducere, conduxi, conductum (3).

reply: respondeo, -ere, respondi, responsum (2).

report: narro (1); nuntio (1).

rest—the rest of: ceterus (bonus).

reward: praemium (2, *n*).

river: flumen, fluminis (3, *n*).

road: via (1, *f*).

rock: saxum (2, *n*).

Roman *noun:* Romanus (2, *m*);
      adj: Romanus (bonus).

Rome: Roma (1, *f*).

rose: rosa (1, *f*).

round: circum (*prep + acc*).

rule: rego, regere, rexi, rectum (3).

run: curro, -ere, cucurri (3).
  run forward: procurro, -ere, procurri (3).

rush: ruo, ruere, rui (3).

S

sail: navigo (1).

sailor: nauta (1, *m*).

sand: harena (1, *f*).

savage: saevus (bonus).

save: servo (1).

say: dico, dicere, dixi, dictum (3).

school: ludus (2, *m*).

Scot: Caledonius (2, *m*).

sea: mare, maris (3, *n*).

secutor: secutor, secutoris (3, *m*).

see: video, videre, vidi, visum (2).

seek: peto, petere, petivi, petitum (3).

seize: rapio, rapere, rapui, raptum (3½).

sell: vendo, vendere, vendidi, venditum (3).

senator: senator, senatoris (3, *m*).

send: mitto, mittere, misi, missum (3).

serious: gravis (tristis).

shield: scutum (2, *n*).

ship: navis, navis (3, *f*).

shop: taberna (1, *f*).

short: brevis (tristis).

shout: *verb:* clamo (1).
      noun: clamor, -oris, (*m*).

show: demonstro (1).

shut: claudo, claudere, clausi, clausum (3).
  shut up: taceo (2).

sick: aeger (niger).

sight: conspicio (3½).

sign: signum (2, *n*).
signal: signum (2, *n*).
silent— am silent: taceo (2).
sing: canto (1).
sister: soror, sororis (3, *f*).
sit: sedeo, sedere, sedi (2).
slave: servus (2, *m*).
slave girl: ancilla (1, *f*).
slay: occido, -ere, occidi, occisum (3).
sleep: dormio (4).
slowly: lente (*adv*).
small: parvus (bonus).
smile: rideo, -ere, risi (2).
so: tam (*adv*).
soft: tener.
soldier: miles, militis (3, *m*).
son: filius (2, *m*).
song: carmen, carminis (3, *n*).
soon: mox (*adv*).
sound: sonus (2, *m*).
spear: telum (2, *n*).
spider: aranea (1, *f*).
Spurius: Spurius (2, *m*).
stay; maneo, -ere, mansi (2).
stand: sto, stare, steti (1).
storm: tempestas, tempestatis (3, *f*).
story: fabula (1, *f*).
street: via (1, *f*).
study: tablinum (2, *n*).
stupid: stultus (bonus).
suddenly: subito (*adv*).
supper: cena (1, *f*).
surely: nonne *or* num (*advs*).
swift: velox, velocis (felix).
swim: nato (1).
sword: gladius (2, *m*).

T

table: mensa (1, *f*).
task: opus, operis (3, *n*).
take *catch:* capio, capere, cepi, captum $(3\frac{1}{2})$.
  lead: duco, ducere, duxi, ductum (3).
  lift: sumo, sumere, sumpsi, sumptum (3).

teach: doceo, docere, docui, doctum (2).
tell: dico, dicere, dixi, dictum (3).
temple: templum (2, *n*).
tender: tener.
than: quam (*conj*).
that: is *or* ille.
their (own): suus (bonus).
then: inde (*adv*).
there: ibi (*adv*).
thing: res (5, *f*).
this: hic.
though: quamquam (*conj*).
throat: iugulum (2, *n*).
through: per (*prep+acc*).
throw: conicio, conicere, conieci, coniectum $(3\frac{1}{2})$.
thrust: inmitto, inmittere, inmisi, inmissum (3).
time: tempus, temporis (3, *n*).
tired: fessus (bonus).
Titus: Titus (2, *m*).
to: ad (*prep+acc*) *or dat*.
today: hodie (*adv*).
toga: toga (1, *f*).
tomorrow: cras (*adv*).
too much: nimis (*indecl*).
touch: tango, tangere, tetigi, tactum (3).
town: oppidum (2, *n*).
tree: arbor, arboris (3, *f*).
tribune: tribunus (2, *m*).
Trojan *noun:* Troianus (2, *m*).
    adj: Troianus (bonus).
try: tempto (1).
Tullus: Tullus (2, *m*).
tunic: tunica (1, *f*).

U

under: sub (*prep+abl*).
understand: intellego, -ere, intellexi (3).
unhealthy: pestilens (ingens).
used to: *use imperfect*.

V

vain—in vain: frustra (*adv*).
very much: magnopere (*adv*).

viper: vipera (1, *f*).
voice: vox, vocis (3, *f*).

W

wage: gero, gerere, gessi, gestum (3).
wait (for): exspecto (1).
walk: ambulo (1).
wall: murus (2, *m*).
want: cupio, cupere, cupivi, cupitum (3½).
war: bellum (2, *n*).
warn: moneo (2).
watch *verb:* specto (1);
    noun: vigilia (1, *f*).
water: aqua (1, *f*).
waterfall: cataracta (1, *f*).
weapon: telum (2, *n*).
wear: gero, -ere, gessi (3).
weather: tempestas, tempestatis (3, *f*).
weep: fleo, flere, flevi (2).
wet: madidus (bonus).
what?: quid?
when: ubi (*adv* or *conj*);
  in questions: quando (*adv*).
where: ubi (*adv*).
while: dum (*conj*).
who?: quis?
whole: totus (unus).

why?: cur? (*adv*).
win: vinco, vincere, vici (3).
wine: vinum (2, *n*).
wing (of army): cornu (4, *n*).
winter: hiems, hiemis (3, *f*).
wise: sapiens (ingens).
with: cum (*prep + abl*); *or abl only.*
with difficulty: aegre (*adv*).
woman: femina (1, *f*).
wood: silva (1, *f*).
word: verbum (2, *n*).
work *verb:* laboro (1);
    noun: opus, operis (3, *n*).
wound: *verb:* vulnero (1);
    noun: vulnus, vulneris; (3, *n*).
wretched: miser (tener).
write: scribo, scribere, scripsi, scriptum (3).

Y

year: annus (2, *m*).
yesterday: heri (*adv*).
you: tu; *plural:* vos.
young man: iuvenis, iuvenis (3, *m*).
your: tuus (bonus); vester (niger).